Apps for Librarians

Apps for Librarians

Using the Best Mobile Technology to Educate, Create, and Engage

Nicole Hennig

 LIBRARIES UNLIMITED

AN IMPRINT OF ABC-CLIO, LLC
Santa Barbara, California • Denver, Colorado • Oxford, England

Library of Congress Cataloging-in-Publication Data

Hennig, Nicole.
  Apps for librarians : using the best mobile technology to educate, create, and engage / Nicole Hennig.
     pages cm
  Includes bibliographical references and index.
     ISBN 978–1–61069–530–5 (paperback) — ISBN 978–1–61069–531–2 (ebook) 1. Mobile communication systems—Library applications. 2. Library science—Computer programs. 3. Application software—Directories. I. Title.
  Z680.5.H46   2014
  025.00285—dc23   2014017723

ISBN: 978–1–61069–530–5
EISBN: 978–1–61069–531–2

18 17 16 15   4 5 6

This book is also available on the World Wide Web as an eBook.
Visit www.abc-clio.com for details.

Libraries Unlimited
An Imprint of ABC-CLIO, LLC

ABC-CLIO, LLC
130 Cremona Drive, P.O. Box 1911
Santa Barbara, California 93116-1911

This book is printed on acid-free paper ∞

Manufactured in the United States of America

Contents

Acknowledgments

I would like to thank my friends and colleagues from the MIT Libraries who supported my enthusiasm and evangelism for the world of mobile apps from the day the first iPhone was announced. I'd especially like to thank the user experience librarians, who are fabulous UX professionals: Darcy Duke, Melissa Feiden, Remlee Green, Stephanie Hartman, Lisa Horowitz, and Georgiana McReynolds.

I'd also like to thank all of the students who've participated in my online courses: *Apps for Librarians and Educators,* and *The Book as iPad App* (http://nicolehennig.com/courses/). Your feedback and enthusiasm for the topic helped me continually improve the course and inspired me to write this book.

Introduction

Why a Book?

You've probably picked up this book because you're interested in learning more about apps and finding the best ways to use them in your library. If so, you've come to the right place!

Apps are everywhere these days and it can be overwhelming to know where to start and how to find the best-quality apps. This book will give you a solid foundation. If you don't have one yet, it's recommended that you get a mobile device[1] and try many of the apps yourself, using this book as a guide. You'll learn what's technically possible with mobile apps and devices, which quality apps have become "core," how to keep up with new apps and find quality reviews, what to include when reviewing apps, and see examples of how libraries are using apps in creative ways.

Some say that it's best to start with understanding what your users need, rather than starting with particular technologies. In my experience, it's good to understand both—keep exploring new technologies, so that you can match what's possible to what your users need. Often people will not know they "need" something until it exists and shows amazing potential for improving their lives.[2]

Who This Book Is For

This book is for librarians from all types of institutions who would like to learn about the best mobile apps for their own professional use and for recommending to users. It's especially appropriate for those who offer workshops to their communities and who review and select apps.

If you are new to mobile computing with apps, or if you've used only the preinstalled apps on your smartphone or tablet, then this book is for you. It will save you the time of wading through the millions of apps available in today's app stores (of varying quality), and point you to the very best apps in several areas important for education, the workplace, and professional development.

Platforms Included

This book will focus primarily on apps for Apple's iOS and secondarily for Google's Android platforms. Many of these apps are available on both platforms, and for those that are for iOS only, I'll recommend alternatives for Android users. Much of the innovation in the app world is happening first on Apple's platform. This is currently where the money is for developers so that's why they usually develop there first.

Conventions Used

For each app, the following are included:

- Developer
- Platforms
- Version
- Price

Keep in mind that prices change frequently and apps go on sale from time to time, so it's best to look in the app stores for current prices.

Platforms

For each app, I've listed the platforms it runs on. For example:

- Android: Google's mobile platform (specific Android versions not listed)
- iOS: Apple's mobile platform for iPad, iPhone, and iPod Touch
- iOS (universal): Apple's term for apps that are optimized for all screen sizes, including iPad
- iOS (iPad only): Apps that are designed only for the iPad

Some iOS apps are offered with different versions for iPhone and iPad (usually with different prices). Some iOS apps are *not* universal, but they can run on iPads in a small window, which you can tap on to double the size.

Since apps are updated frequently, I've listed the version number for each app at the time of writing. Version numbers in this book are for iOS only. Most apps keep the same core features over time, and with updates, the developers fix bugs or add new features. Depending on when you're reading this, a newer version of the app may exist with more features. It's also possible that an app may have been purchased by another company (Google purchased Quickoffice, for example), which means that sometimes the features will be changed. Once in a while, an app will be discontinued entirely and removed from the app stores.

Other Platforms

Some of the apps in this book are available for other mobile and desktop platforms, though they won't be listed here. Follow the link to the developer's website if you are interested in finding out about the availability of these apps on other platforms.

What This Book Doesn't Cover

This book will not cover the practical aspects of loaning iPads or other mobile devices in libraries, or the copyright issues involved. That could be a topic for a whole book. Instead, we'll focus on the apps and how they can be used.

There is a very good online course offered from time to time about this topic by Rebecca K. Miller, Carolyn Meir, and Heather Moorefield-Lang of Virginia Tech. Follow their blog, *iPad and Tablets in Libraries*, for more details: http://tabletsinlibraries.tumblr.com/.

Companion Website

For updates to the information in this book, see the companion website: http://apps4librarians.com/thebook/.

I'd love to hear from you—send your comments and suggestions for future editions, along with stories of how you are using mobile apps in your library: http://nicolehennig.com/contact-me/.

Notes

1. See the buying guide from Macrumors for excellent advice on timing your purchase of Apple devices, so you don't buy a new iPad right before a new version is released: http://buyersguide.macrumors.com/.

2. For an inspiring example, see "Re-Enabled: iOS's Impact on Those with Impairments Isn't Just a Marketing Slide; It's Profound" at http://the-magazine.org/9/re-enabled.

CHAPTER 1

Mobile Is Here to Stay

Statistics on Mobile App Use

You may wonder if the app world is just another flashy technology that will be here today and gone tomorrow. I'd like to give evidence for why mobile technology is here to stay, and also why it's a beneficial development for students and professionals of all ages and abilities.

Pew Internet Research reports that 56 percent of adults in the United States have smartphones and 91 percent have some kind of cell phone.[1] As for tablets, Pew Internet in 2013 reports that for the first time, 34 percent of adults in the United States own a tablet computer. That's almost twice as many as the 18 percent who owned one during the previous year.[2]

Not only adults, but teens are using these technologies. According to the report "Teens and Technology 2013," 37 percent of all teens ages 12–17 have smartphones, up from just 23 percent in 2011. One in four teens are "cell-mostly" Internet users—they mostly go online using their phone.[3]

Statistics from ComScore also show that people in the United States are using mobile apps more than the mobile web. The split is about 80 percent of time on apps versus 20 percent of time on mobile websites.[4]

Another interesting development is that mobile Internet use is beginning to overtake desktop use.[5] According to a 2013 article in the *Economist*, the Internet is on its way to becoming a mostly mobile medium. Soon there will be more mobile users than desktop users.[6]

As you'll see when you spend time getting to know the wide variety of mobile apps, mobile devices, and their unique capabilities, this is a mobile era. That's why it's important for librarians to become "app-literate," so we can evolve our work to stay relevant in this mobile world.

Natural User Interfaces

One of the most important developments is the move away from GUIs (graphical user interfaces) and toward NUIs (natural user interfaces). These are touch-based, speech-based, and camera-based interfaces that resemble the physical world in how they work. Touching an icon or other element and dragging it across the screen is something that toddlers and the elderly are able to figure out and understand quickly.

On the other hand, graphical user interfaces are abstract metaphors using the idea of a desktop, folders, and trash cans. They use hierarchical menu systems with pointing devices (mice and trackpads) that are removed from the natural feel of objects in the real world. We take that abstraction for granted, but it's something we had to learn at one time in order to use today's desktop computers.

If you're interested in learning more about NUIs, read the excellent book *Brave NUI World: Designing Natural User Interfaces for Touch and Gesture* by Daniel Wigdor, available at http://www.worldcat.org/oclc/681501624.

Mobile Devices Are Enabling Better Learning Experiences

Now that iPads have been in use for a few years, there are studies showing that the use of tablets is improving learning.

In a survey by the Pearson Foundation, a majority of college students and high school seniors agreed that tablets help them study more efficiently (66% and 64%) and perform better in classes (64% and 63%).[7]

A study conducted in Auburn, Maine, showed that kindergarten students using iPads scored much higher on literacy tests than those who didn't use iPads.[8]

At Northdale Middle School in Coon Rapids, Minnesota, iPads in the classroom have led to increased engagement among disabled students and have accelerated their learning and comprehension.[9]

For more study results, see Ashley Wainwright's "8 Studies Show iPads in the Classroom Improve Education."[10]

Mobile Apps Are Improving Life for Those with Special Needs

Mobile devices, especially those designed by Apple, include many accessibility features. These include a long list of settings and tools that help with vision, hearing, physical motor skills, learning, and literacy.

For example, Apple's Voice Over is a screen reader that lets you know what's happening on the screen to help you navigate. Speak Selection can be used to read text on your screen aloud. Dictation lets you talk into the microphone and have your words converted to text. Zoom is a built-in magnifier that works anywhere on Apple's devices, including within all the apps. Face Time video calls are great for the deaf or hearing impaired. You can see each other's face and hands while you talk. The iTunes store contains many movies, TV shows, and podcasts with closed captioning available. There are vibrating alerts or LED light flashes for incoming calls and messages.

For more details about these features, see the section later in this book: Apple's Accessibility Features for Mobile Devices.

A great source of individual stories of how apps are helping those with special needs is the website Bridging Apps: Bridging the Gaps between Technology and People with Disabilities. Take a look at their "success stories" for inspiration and ideas: http://bridgingapps.org/.

The Digital Divide

Lacking the resources to afford these technologies is a big issue. However, there is reason for optimism.

Compared to the cost of desktop and laptop computers, mobile devices are generally less expensive. An iPod Touch, for example, can run the vast majority of apps that the iPhone can; it just lacks a phone (and expensive monthly plans). These can be purchased used or refurbished for a very low price. The iPad mini is another good option in its smallest configuration, especially if purchased used or refurbished. (See the Apple Store online for refurbished models.)[11]

Not only that, there are special programs, grants, donations, and a growing trend of school systems providing iPads and mobile technology to all students.

Special Programs

The EveryoneOn program (http://www.everyoneon.org) is a wonderful example of a program designed to help bridge the digital divide. They offer low-cost devices and Internet service, as well as digital literacy–training programs around the United States. They are aiming to help the estimated 100 million Americans who don't have broadband connections at home and also the 62 million who don't use the Internet at all.[12]

School Districts Providing iPads

More and more we're hearing about schools that are providing iPads for every student. You've probably seen headlines like these:

- "640,000 LA Students Will Get Free iPads by 2014."[13]

- "Illinois School District to Give Up to 7,000 Apple iPads to Students."[14]

- "Miami-Dade to Ensure Every Student Has Digital Device by 2015."[15]

Giving iPads to everyone is not an answer to all the problems of today's classrooms, but it does help to get students excited about learning[16] and gives teachers opportunities for creating interactive lessons involving content creation on the iPad.[17]

The initiative in the Los Angeles public schools to give iPads to all students has been criticized as costly and inept, but the criticism is seen by some as hostility toward giving poor students access to the best tools. After some problems with their pilot program, the initiative is moving forward with support from teachers who are having successes in the classroom with iPads.[18]

Donations and Grants

Another way to help bridge the divide is by donations and grants for educational institutions. In 2011 Apple was donating iPads to the Teach for America program for teachers in low-income areas. Now Apple donates to foundations that provide grants for iPads.[19]

Often grants designed to help students with special needs will fund mobile technologies. For information on where to apply, see "iPad Grants to Improve Learning: A Guide to Where to Look for Grants."[20] The "Grants Guys" recommend using Donors Choose (http://www.donorschoose.org/) as a way to fund iPads for classrooms.[21]

What's Happening Internationally

There are many interesting programs happening outside of the United States as well. For example, in Thailand the One Tablet PC Per Child campaign spent $32.8 million (1.02 billion Thai Baht) to provide tablets to students in their schools.[22]

In Turkey, they have launched a project called Movement to Increase Opportunities and Technology (FATIH), which funds tablets in Turkish schools.[23]

In a post on the EduTech blog from the World Bank, there is a great summary of educational laptop and tablet projects in 10 countries, including the United States, Uruguay, Thailand, Peru, Kenya, Turkey, India, Argentina, and Portugal.[24]

Opportunities for Successful Initiatives

The digital divide is definitely not closed, but at least there is attention to this issue and work to help bridge the gap. Of course some of these programs have been criticized for throwing technology at a problem without planning, but there are many thoughtful resources and plans available for creating successful iPad initiatives in schools. The best recommend providing training programs for teachers, building content around the technology, and communicating transparently to all stakeholders.[25]

Libraries and librarians from school, public, and academic libraries have opportunities to provide information resources in these areas for their communities.

New Roles for Libraries and Librarians

You may be familiar with the *Atlas of New Librarianship* by R. David Lankes (Cambridge, MA: MIT Press, 2011, http://www.worldcat.org/oclc/641998875). In it, he states:

> The mission of librarians is to improve society through facilitating knowledge creation in their communities. (http://www.newlibrarianship.org/wordpress/)

If you haven't yet read his book, it's highly recommended for fresh, deep thinking about the profession of librarianship.

If you believe in that mission statement as I do, then getting involved with mobile apps is one way to help facilitate knowledge creation in our communities, since apps are tools for knowledge creation (as you will see in the app descriptions throughout this book).

Libraries are already beginning to do this by offering workshops about apps, making iPads available with interactive eBooks on them, negotiating with publishers for better eBook-lending deals, offering workshops for people who want to self-publish interactive iPad eBooks, contributing app reviews to the professional literature, and more.

I hope that this book will inspire you with ideas for getting involved with the world of mobile apps, both for your own professional use and as a way for your library to facilitate knowledge creation in your communities.

Notes

1. "Smartphone Ownership 2013," http://www.pewinternet.org/Reports/2013/Smartphone-Ownership-2013.aspx.

2. "Tablet Ownership 2013," http://www.pewinternet.org/Reports/2013/Tablet-Ownership-2013.aspx.

3. "Report: Teens and Technology 2013," http://youthandmedia.org/report-teens-and-tech/.

4. "Mobile Web Accounts for Just a Fifth of Time Spent on Devices, Apps Reign Supreme," http://www.tnooz.com/2012/05/09/mobile/mobile-web-accounts-for-just-a-fifth-of-time-spent-on-devices-apps-reign-supreme/.

5. "U.S. Time on Mobile to Overtake Desktop," http://www.emarketer.com/Article/US-Time-Spent-on-Mobile-Overtake-Desktop/1010095.

6. "Live and Unplugged: In 2013 the Internet Will Become a Mostly Mobile Medium. Who Will Be the Winners and Losers?" http://www.economist.com/news/21566417-2013-internet-will-become-mostly-mobile-medium-who-will-be-winners-and-losers-live-and.

7. "Pearson Foundation Survey on Students and Tablets 2012," http://www.pearsonfoundation.org/downloads/PF_Tablet_Survey_Summary_2012.pdf.

8. "iPad-Equipped Medical School Class Scores 23 Percent Higher on Exams," http://mobihealthnews.com/20311/ipad-equipped-medical-school-class-scores-23-percent-higher-on-exams/.

9. "iPads Improve Special Education at Coon Rapids School," http://www.startribune.com/local/north/179835811.html.

10. "8 Studies Show iPads in the Classroom Improve Education," http://www.securedgenetworks.com/secure-edge-networks-blog/bid/86775/8-Studies-Show-iPads-in-the-Classroom-Improve-Education.

11. Apple's refurbished iPads can be an excellent choice: http://store.apple.com/us/browse/home/specialdeals/ipad.

12. "Internet Access for All: A New Program Targets Low-Income Students," http://blogs.kqed.org/mindshift/2013/03/internet-access-for-everyone-a-new-program-targets-low-income-students/.

13. "640,000 LA Students Will Get Free iPads by 2014," http://www.nbclosangeles.com/news/local/Every-LA-Student-Will-Get-Free-iPad-by-2014-217090561.html.

14. "Illinois School District to Give Up to 7,000 Apple iPads to Students," http://macdailynews.com/2013/02/17/illinois-school-district-to-give-up-to-7000-apple-ipads-to-students/.

15. "Miami-Dade to Ensure Every Student Has Digital Device by 2015," http://www.miamiherald.com/2013/06/19/3460509/miami-dade-to-ensure-every-student.html.

16. "Three student successes with iPads," http://digital.hechingerreport.org/content/three-student-successes-with-ipads_973/.

17. EdTech Teacher is a good resource for teachers developing lesson plans using iPads in schools: http://edtechteacher.org/innovative/.

18. "Despite Bad Press, LAUSD's iPad Curriculum Is Impressing Educators," http://www.laweekly.com/2013-12-19/news/lausd-ipad-pearson-common-core/.

19. "Apple Donates Thousands of iPads to Teachers in Low-Income Areas," http://www.mactrast.com/2011/09/apple-donates-thousands-of-ipads-to-volunteer-teachers-in-low-income-areas/.

20. "iPad Grants to Improve Learning," http://www.squidoo.com/ipad-grants.

21. "How to Find Grants for iPads in the Classroom," http://grantsguys.com/grants-for-ipads-in-the-classroom/.

22. "Thailand Signs the World's Largest Educational Tablet Distribution Deal," http://www.digitaltrends.com/international/thailand-signs-the-worlds-largest-educational-tablet-distribution-deal/.

23. Tablets to Students to Improve Quality and Productivity," http://www.dailysabah.com/education/2014/02/27/tablets-to-students-to-improve-quality-and-productivity.

24. "Big Educational Laptop and Tablet Projects: Ten Countries to Learn From," http://blogs.worldbank.org/edutech/big-educational-laptop-and-tablet-projects-ten-countries.

25. "Keys to a Successful iPad Initiative," http://mobilelearningcoach.com/keys-to-a-successful-ipad-iniative/.

CHAPTER 2

Apps for Reading

Reading eBooks

Kindle

- Developer: Amazon, http://www.amazon.com/
- Version: 4.0
- Platforms: Android, iOS (universal)
- Price: free

The Kindle app remains one of the best apps for reading eBooks, and it's available free for multiple platforms and devices. Of course, Amazon has a huge catalog of available titles, and the eBooks are usually cheaper than print versions. Free samples of each book are available help you decide which books to purchase.

Your titles are stored in Amazon's cloud, which gives you instant access to all your books from anywhere, and you can add or remove them from your device at any time. Kindle syncs between devices, so if you own an iPhone and iPad, an Android device and a PC, or any other combination, it will remember where you left off reading when you switch devices. Font size and other layout aspects are adjustable, which makes for easy reading, even on small screens.

You can view popular notes and highlights, and share your own on Facebook and Twitter. A built-in dictionary is included with the app, making it easy to look up any word as you read. When an author updates a title, you get notified and can freely download the updated edition—especially useful for subjects that are rapidly changing.

If your library subscribes to Overdrive, your users can borrow books on that service and have them sent to their Kindle app (for many titles).

See Amazon's "Borrow Books from a Public Library" page for details.[1]

Example

The New York Public Library has helpful instructions for patrons in "Library Books on Kindle: A Visual Walkthrough."[2] These instructions work for the Kindle mobile apps as well as for Kindle e-reading devices.

Audience

Anyone who likes to read many books, carry their books with them on mobile devices, and who wants to take advantage of a built-in dictionary and easy highlighting.

Other Apps Worth Trying

- NOOK: http://www.barnesandnoble.com/u/nook-mobile-apps/379003593/. Android, iOS (universal). Barnes and Noble's app for reading eBooks.

- Kobo Reading App: http://www.kobo.com/apps. Android, iOS (universal). Official app of the Canadian bookseller Kobo. Has a well-designed user interface.

- Google Play Books: https://play.google.com/store/apps/details?id=com.google.android.apps.books&hl=en. Android, iOS (universal). Google's e-reading app for books from the Google Play store.

iBooks

- Developer: Apple, http://www.apple.com/ibooks/
- Version: 3.1.3
- Platforms: iOS (universal)
- Price: free

Apple's iBooks has some features that are sometimes overlooked but are useful. The app allows you to sort your books into categories on your virtual bookshelf, and also allows for reading PDFs and EPUB-formatted books from sources other than Apple. You can use it on your Mac as well as your iOS devices.

iBooks is also useful because it's designed to read multi-touch textbooks and other interactive books that have been created with Apple's free program, iBooks Author. These books have multimedia content, such as embedded videos, slide shows, quizzes, or 3D images that can be viewed from all angles by spinning around with your finger. See the Made with iBooks Author section in this chapter for some examples.

Audience

Students and professors who want to use interactive books made with iBooks Author (textbooks and more). Anyone who prefers to purchase their eBooks from Apple's iTunes store. Those who would like an app to use as a place to store and organize PDFs or EPUBs purchased from sources other than Apple.

Examples

The University of Minnesota recommends iBooks and mentions useful features for students, such as the ability to add highlights and notes to a central repository. They also recommend the Study Cards feature for creating flashcards from book glossaries.[3]

If you'd like to see the Study Cards feature in action, take a look at this video on YouTube: "Textbooks Study Cards in iBooks 2 for iPad."[4]

Downloading and Reading Free eBooks

MegaReader

- Developer: Inkstone Software, http://www.megareader.net/
- Version: 2.8
- Platforms: iOS (universal), Android version planned for the future
- Price: $0.99

MegaReader is a reader focused on making it easy to get free eBooks for your mobile device. It links to the best free catalogs online, making it easy to download and read more than 2 million titles from sources such as Feedbooks, Smashwords, Project Gutenberg, or Internet Archive.[5]

The app comes with a library of preinstalled titles, so you can try it out right away. When you are online, you can download more eBooks, which are then available to read offline, anytime.

It includes many customization features, including font size, fonts, colors, backgrounds, and more.

It doesn't yet have support for Dropbox within the app, but you can open Dropbox on the web and open files in MegaReader from there. It can import DRM-free EPUB-formatted books. It also integrates with the Instapaper app, which allows you to import text and web pages.

Audience

This app is great for anyone who wants to collect and read the classics of literature and other free eBooks. It's also useful for those with low vision, because of its many customization features, such as large text.

Reading Library eBooks

OverDrive Media Console

- Developer: Overdrive Inc., http://omc.overdrive.com/
- Version: 3.0.3
- Platforms: Android, iOS (universal), and other platforms
- Price: free

The OverDrive app is for reading eBooks or listening to audiobooks that can be downloaded from libraries that subscribe to the OverDrive service. Users can check out titles on their library's website, or browse their library inside the app, and open them to the OverDrive app for reading on the go. When the loan period ends, the book expires from the app. The app requires you to sign in with an Adobe ID (free to get from Adobe via a link in the app).

It has many of the same features that other eBook-reading apps have, such as customizable fonts, sizes, colors, bookmarks, built-in dictionary, and more.

You can also download DRM-free EPUB books from other sources (such as Internet Archive)[6] and read them in this app.

One negative aspect is that the process of searching or browsing your library's OverDrive catalog within the app is not intuitive. It can be clumsy to log in, and to navigate the search and browse features. Once you are past that hurdle, the app works well and serves its purpose, which is to read eBooks on loan from your library.

Audience

Anyone who belongs to a library with the OverDrive service and who wants to borrow library eBooks and read them on mobile devices.

Other Apps Worth Trying

- 3M Cloud Library: http://www.3m.com/us/library/eBook/index.html. Similar to Overdrive. Android, iOS (universal). For an example of a library that offers 3M, see the St. Paul Public Library.[7]

- Bluefire Reader: http://www.bluefirereader.com/white-label-apps.html. Android, iOS (universal). Supports the reading of eBooks with Adobe DRM, which means it can read eBooks from the Overdrive service.

- Oyster—Read Unlimited Books: http://www.oysterbooks.com/. Android, iOS (universal). Unlimited access to more than 500,000 titles for $9.95 per month.

- Scribd—The World's Digital Library: http://www.scribd.com/subscribe. Android, iOS (universal). Unlimited access to more than 300,000 titles for $8.99 per month.

- Hoopla Digital: Android, iOS (universal). https://www.hoopladigital.com/. Download or stream video, music, and audiobooks from your public library.

- Freegal Music: https://itunes.apple.com/us/app/freegal-music/id5080 36345?mt=8. Android, iOS (universal). A music service with streaming and downloading options for libraries to offer to their patrons.

Access to Braille and Talking Books for the Blind

BARD Mobile

- Developer: Library of Congress, http://www.loc.gov/homepage/connect.html

- Version: 1.0

- Platforms: iOS (universal)

- Price: free

The BARD Mobile app provides access to braille and talking books from the NLS (National Library Service for the Blind and Physically Handicapped), Library of Congress.[8] BARD (Braille and Audio Reading Download) contains nearly 50,000 books, magazines, and music scores in audio and braille formats. The app allows blind and physically handicapped users to download these titles directly to their iPhone or iPad for convenient listening. If the device is connected to a Bluetooth braille display,[9] books can be read in braille.

In order to use the app, you must be registered with a library in the NLS network.[10] Those who can't read regular print because of a visual or physical disability can apply for the service by calling 1-800-NLS-READ (1-800-657-7323).

If you have BARD books or magazines on your computer, you can use iTunes file sharing or Dropbox to load them into BARD Mobile. Load them as zip files and BARD Mobile will unpack them automatically.

Before this app was available, people were mailed a talking book machine and/or braille books. Now users of this collection can get instant easy access, using their iPhone, iPad, or iPod. To see or hear a video demonstration of how this app works, watch the YouTube video "BARD Mobile: Introduction" at http://youtu.be/oFocDhTa1FM. To learn more, read the user guide: https://nlsbard.loc.gov/apidocs/BARDMobile.userguide.iOS.1.0.html.

Audience

Blind or physically handicapped users who are members of an NLS library and who want convenient easy access to the collection on their mobile device.

Reading and Annotating Documents

GoodReader 4

- Developer: Yuri Selukoff, http://www.goodreader.com/
- Version: 4.3.0
- Platforms: iOS (universal)
- Price: $6.99

With GoodReader, you can read and annotate just about any type of file, such as plain text, Word, Excel, PowerPoint, images (JPEG, PNG, etc.), video (QuickTime, MP4, etc.), audio (MP3, etc.), or HTML.

GoodReader easily handles massive PDF and TXT files. You can convert a PDF to plain text and make it wrap properly on small screens for ease of reading, and switch back and forth between graphical and text views if you need to see images. Its tabbed interface allows you to view multiple documents in different tabs and switch between them.

GoodReader connects to Dropbox and other cloud storage (OneDrive, SugarSync, Box, and any WebDAV, AFP, SMB, FTP, or SFTP server) for transferring files—or even entire directories—from your desktop computer. Extensive annotation features are included—highlights, pop-up boxes for notes, arrows, freehand drawing, and more.

Audience

Students or anyone who reads a lot of PDF files and needs to annotate them. It's also useful for those with low vision, since you can zoom and wrap text for easy reading.

Examples

Jonathan Messer, a PhD candidate at the College of William and Mary, describes his process for keeping journal articles organized, read, and annotated in "Using GoodReader to Keep Journal Articles Organized, Aid Research."[11]

Linda Braun, a librarian-blogger for YALSA (Young Adult Library Services Association), describes how it's useful both for librarians and for teens who are collecting database articles for homework projects.[12]

Other Apps Worth Trying

- iAnnotate PDF: http://www.branchfire.com/iannotate/. Android, iOS (iPad only). Another good PDF annotation and organization app.

- iBooks: http://www.apple.com/apps/ibooks/. You can also read and organize your PDF files in iBooks. (See full entry in this book.)

Saving Web Pages for Reading Offline

Instapaper

- Developer: Marco Arment, http://www.instapaper.com/iphone

- Version: 5.0.2

- Platforms: iOS (universal), Android

- Price: $3.99

Instapaper is a simple app for saving web pages to read later. But it's also much more. With it, you can create your own collection of saved articles for reading when you are offline. You can read them offline on your mobile devices or online at your desktop computer. Voracious readers will appreciate that you can file your multiple saved readings into folders of your own choosing.

Some of the best features of Instapaper are those that enable a customized reading experience. First, you can adjust the font size and margins, which is helpful for those with impaired vision or for reading in low light. At night you can switch to dark mode for more comfortable reading. This makes reading on small devices like your iPhone very enjoyable. The text wraps properly, so that you don't have to scroll right and left as you might on websites that haven't been optimized for mobile viewing. You can also set a rotation lock, so that the screen won't switch orientations when you don't want it to. This is great for reading in bed.

Other great features include a built-in English dictionary (select a word and tap "define"), posting article links to social media such as Twitter, Tumblr, or Facebook, and browsing through articles that were "liked" by friends or Instapaper's editors.

Instapaper is one of the best ways to save articles while you are doing online research. Note that it works for articles that are free and open on the web, not with articles that are behind a paywall. For those, try using GoodReader (described elsewhere in this book) to save your downloaded PDF files.

Audience

The combination of easy reading features and the fact that you can save so much data for offline reading makes Instapaper a great choice for students or anyone who needs to save a lot of information for reading later.

It's also a great choice for a range of vision problems, since its display is very adjustable to individual needs.

Example

Librarians could use Instapaper for saving professional reading for times when they can focus, such as during a long plane ride.

Other Apps Worth Trying

Both of these apps are very similar to Instapaper and get good reviews. Choosing one is a personal preference.

- Pocket: Save Articles and Videos to View Later. http://getpocket.com/. Android, iOS (universal).
- Readability: http://www.readability.com/apps. Android, iOS (universal).

Reading News via RSS

Reeder 2

- Developer: Silvio Rizzi, http://reederapp.com/ios/
- Version: 2.1.1
- Platforms: iOS (universal)
- Price: $4.99

Reeder is a useful tool for people who subscribe to many RSS feeds. Before Google Reader was closed, Reeder was a favorite app of many as a front end for it. Now Reeder is a front end to Feedbin, Feedly, Feed Wrangler, and Readability.

It's a useful app for reading feeds on a small screen. You can change the font size, switch to the website view to see the original look of the article, or send it out to Safari to use your bookmarks or other sharing tools.

Many sharing options are available from Reeder: Delicious, Instapaper, Readbility, Pocket, Evernote, Pinboard, Twitter, Facebook, Buffer, and more. This makes it a very useful way to find material for your social media feeds. It's very easy to tweet articles directly from this app. You can also easily e-mail a link or entire article.

Audience

Reeder is useful for those who follow many news feeds and like to have one place to keep up with everything. It's also useful for those who need content to add to social media, since it's so convenient to send items to Twitter and other sites.

Other Apps Worth Trying

- Feedly: http://blog.feedly.com/mobile/. Another very good RSS reader.

Reading Magazines

Zinio—5,000 + Digital Magazines

- Developer: Zinio LLC, http://www.zinio.com/www/apps/desktop.jsp
- Version: 2.5.8
- Platforms: Android, iOS (universal)
- Price: free; pay for individual magazines within the app

Zinio is a convenient way to read magazines on your mobile device. It's especially nice for reading on iPads, with their larger screens. After you set up an account on Zinio, you can purchase individual magazines or subscribe by the year. Prices are similar to what they would be on news-stands. For example, *Discover* magazine is $19.19 for a one-year sub-scription (10 issues) or $5.99 for 1 issue.

Zinio contains a large variety of magazines (more than 5,000) in many topic areas, everything from well-known publications, such as the *Economist* or *Harvard Business Review*, to popular titles, such as *Elle Décor* or *Martha Stewart Living*. It also contains local publications, such as *Chicago Magazine*, and indie-press titles, like *Broken Pencil*. There are also many publications in German, French, Spanish, Italian, Portuguese, Russian, and other languages.

You can browse or search through available publications and read sample articles for free. Your purchases are stored in a library on Zinio's site, so you can delete magazines from your device in order to save space, and easily download them again later if you like. You can read your magazines when you are offline and sync them between devices when you are online.

The magazines display with the same layout as they do in print. A nice feature is the ability to zoom in to the part of the page you are reading. This is great for people who need reading glasses or have vision problems. The zoom feature is easy to adjust and can make tiny print very large. Since mobile devices have easy ways to capture their screens, a useful way to save tidbits of information is to zoom in and capture part of the page you are reading.[13]

Zinio also has a feature for individuals called Z-pass, where you can choose three magazines to subscribe to for a total cost of $5 per month.

Libraries can make Zinio titles available to their users through a service offered by Recorded Books and Zinio. According to Michael Kelly in "Recorded Books and Zinio Debuting Digital Magazine Newsstand for U.S. Libraries," "Multiple patrons can read the same title simultaneously, and libraries pay per title in addition to a tiered platform fee that is calculated based on annual material circulations."[14]

Audience

Zinio is perfect for magazine lovers, especially anyone with vision problems, or people who are traveling and would like to load their iPad with several magazines for the trip.

Example

West Hartford Libraries offers a well-designed FAQ for their library users about Zinio: http://www.westhartfordlibrary.org/books_dvds_more/zinio.

Other Apps Worth Trying

- Next Issue: http://www.nextissue.com/. Android, iOS (universal). Contains fewer magazines than Zinio (about 100), but you can read all of them for a small monthly fee ("Netflix" for magazines). For a comparison review, see "Newsstand vs. Next Issue vs. Zinio: Magazine Subscription Apps for iPad Shootout!"[15]

Reading Magazines and Newspapers

Apple Newsstand

- Developer: Apple, https://itunes.apple.com/us/genre/ios-newsstand/id6021?mt=8

- Platforms: iOS (universal)

- Price: free, pay for magazines inside the app individually

Apple Newsstand is a built-in application for downloading and reading magazines and newspapers. It functions more like a folder than an app, since it's a container for other apps, such as the *New York Times* or *Macworld*. Using it, you can browse and download free samples of magazines and newspapers, and subscribe to the ones you like. The fact that each publication is an individual app inside of Newsstand can be slightly confusing, since you need to hit the "home" button to go back to your virtual "shelves" and select another title.

One of the best things about this app is the large number of publications available, more than other magazine apps at the time of this writing (Zinio or Next Issue). A complete list is available on Apple's website.[16] Most publications have free samples available. You can purchase an individual issue or an ongoing subscription. That becomes an "in-app purchase,"[17] which is convenient, since Apple already has your credit card information on file. For each publication, you can choose to auto-renew or not, and Apple sends a reminder e-mail when it's close to renewal time, so you can easily change your preferences.

Apple leaves it up to each publisher to design the reading experience. That means that some publications can be confusing to navigate, while others have a wonderful user experience. To see a well-designed publication, try *Popular Mechanics* (free sample available).[18] The iPad version contains interactive diagrams, animations, and videos, with links to additional content online.

One thing that's not designed well is the method for searching for publications. After you tap on "store" in the Newsstand app, you are taken to the Newsstand section of the app store, which you can browse. But when you search, you are searching the entire app store, including all types of apps, not just magazines. Another thing to be aware of is that some Newsstand publications are available only for iPad, not iPhone or iPod Touch.

Audience

Newsstand is great for those with vision problems, since you can easily zoom in on what you're reading. It's also good for those who like the convenience of purchasing from Apple, with no need to set up an account on another site (like Zinio). Depending on which publications you want to read, Newsstand might be the only source of reading those magazines on your iPad. It does cost more than package deals like those offered by Next Issue,[19] but has many more publications available.

As of this writing, Newsstand does not seem to be available for libraries to offer to their users. Zinio is available for that purpose.

Finding Book Reviews

YALSA's Teen Book Finder

- Developer: American Library Association, http://www.ala.org/yalsa/products/teenbookfinder
- Version: 1.1
- Platforms: iOS (Android version planned for late 2014)
- Price: free

This app makes it easy to browse YALSA's awards and lists on your mobile device. YALSA is the Young Adult Library Services Association, a division of the American Library Association.

The app opens with a "hot picks" section, showing three titles, refreshed daily. You can search and browse by title, author, genre, year, award, and booklist. When you select a title, you can read a brief capsule review, see which lists it has appeared on, see which awards it has won, and add it to your own "favorites" list.

You can also share the title via Facebook or Twitter. If you click the "find it" button, it shows libraries near you that have the book. This feature is based on OCLC's WorldCat[20] search, so only those libraries who are in WorldCat will appear.

Audience

This app is great both for teens and for the librarians who support them. It's also useful for parents or anyone who wants to find recommended reading for young adults.

Sharing Your Reading

Goodreads

- Developer: Goodreads, http://www.goodreads.com/
- Version: 2.3
- Platforms: Android, iOS (universal)
- Price: free

Goodreads is a free social media site for sharing information about books: books you're reading, books you've read, books you want to read, and more. The Goodreads app is a convenient way to participate in the site. With it you can search for books, add them to your virtual shelves, update your profile, view the activity of your friends, download and read free eBooks from public domain collections, join and view groups, browse books by genre, and more.

An additional feature contained in the app, which you can't do on your desktop or laptop, is a book-scanning feature. Scan the barcode and it will find the book on Goodreads for you to add to your shelves.

As of July 2013, Goodreads has 20 million members.[21] Its database is created and edited by the members of Goodreads. If you want to help update and improve the database, you can join the group for librarians. They invite librarians and non-librarians to join the group, where they can comment or request changes to book records in order to improve their catalog.[22]

Audience

Goodreads is for book lovers everywhere who enjoy sharing opinions about books and finding new ideas for books to read.

Example

Travis Jonker, a school librarian, describes how he uses Goodreads in this article: "Get to Know Goodreads: Share This Primer to the Social Reading Site and Help Teachers and Kids Connect with Great Books."[23] He talks about how Goodreads helps him keep up with the latest in book publishing for kids.

Other Apps Worth Trying

- iBookshelf: https://itunes.apple.com/us/app/ibookshelf/id314982342?mt=8. iOS (universal). Create a database of your personal book collection.

- Book Crawler: http://www.chiisai.com/j25/. iOS (universal). Another app for creating a database of your own book collection.

Interactive Multi-touch Book Apps

The world of books and the world of apps is overlapping. Many books are now published as individual apps with multimedia features that go beyond what's possible within traditional e-reading apps, such as Kindle.

The following is a brief list of "book apps" that show the range of possibilities for education because of their interactive features. They take advantage of mobile device features such as speech input, social interaction, multi-touch visuals, geolocation, and more.

To learn more about book apps, sign up for my online course, The Book as iPad App.[24] See also the free resource guide[25] for the course, which includes a longer list of book apps, and additional resources, such as blogs, publishers to watch, libraries to watch, and platforms for creating your own interactive books.

Specialized Encyclopedia

London: A City through Time

- Developer: Heuristic Media, http://www.heuristicmedia.tv/london-a-city-through-time.php

- Version: 1.5

- Platforms: iOS

- Price: $13.99 for iPad, $6.99 for iPhone

This is a wonderful, full-featured app for exploring the history of London. It's beautifully designed and has won several awards.[26] It contains the entire text of the *London Encyclopedia*, with more than 6,000 articles.[27] The developers collaborated with the Museum of London, so it includes content from the museum, such as photos of objects that you can spin around by touching the iPad in order to see all sides of the artifact.

It also contains more than 2,000 rare prints and photos, 35 video documentaries from the archives of the Pathé Movie Library, panoramic photos of present-day London neighborhoods, and audio walking tours. This huge amount of content is nicely organized for a wonderful user experience.

There are several ways to browse, including by timeline, map, subject, or person. The timeline has several layers that you can scroll horizontally in order to view information by century, year, or reign of kings and queens. There is sample music you can listen to for each century. For selected periods of time, the *Illustrated London News* is included, with sample articles. To try it, select 1922 and you'll find an image of the newspaper article about the telephone rotary dial and how to use it. It's fun to zoom in on the article, making it easy to read the tiny print and see the illustrations.

When browsing by map, the app recognizes where you are, so if you are in London, you can browse the entries nearby. No matter where you are, you can zoom in to any area of the map and select icons representing places, such as the Tate Modern. The icons lead to the encyclopedia entries for that place. The map can be toggled between street and satellite views. There are panoramic photos included for many places. There is also a section organized by Tube station map, so you can read about the historical places near each station.

In another section, notable people discuss their favorite spots in London. You can also search the app and limit to keywords, titles of articles, or people.

Audience

This app is useful for anyone interested in the history of London, or present-day London. It's a multimedia reference tool that can do more than a printed book can. One could imagine libraries having iPads for use in the library, loaded with this type of reference app.

Example

If your library offers iPads for use in the library, one could imagine installing a set of specialized reference apps on them, like this one. Users could browse, read, and listen with headphones to information about the history of London.

Astronomy Guide

Solar Walk—Planets of the Solar System

- Developer: Vito Technology Inc., http://www.vitotechnology.com/solar-walk.html
- Version: 2.2.4
- Platforms: Android, iOS (universal)
- Price: $2.99

Solar Walk is an interactive 3D model of the solar system and the Milky Way galaxy. Give this app a try to see why it gets rave reviews—the visuals are wonderful and it's fun to use. Browse by using multi-touch gestures to zoom in or out to different planets. Search by tapping on the "search" button, then select a planet, a comet, or dwarf planets and asteroids.

For example, select Saturn and the app will zoom to Saturn, showing its rings and moons. Spin around or zoom in to view it from different perspectives. Tap on the "i" button to bring up screens with background information, facts and figures, and internal structure of the planet (with visuals). Scroll through photos at the bottom to see interesting photos of the planet and its surface.

Tapping on the extras choice brings up a set of built-in short movies. These are worth watching and are on topics such as size comparisons, Earth's cycles, solar eclipse, or tidal phenomena.

The shop includes in-app purchases ($0.99 each) for more features, such as Apollo 17, the launch of Hubble, and more. Look for the Educator's Pack to find a link to a brief survey that will result in a coupon code (sent to you within about five working days) that gives you extras for free.

A feature worth trying is this: search for Earth, then tap on one of the satellites in orbit. Or go to the "missions" tab in the search area and select "ISS" (International Space Station). Drag the satellite so Earth is visible under it, then slide the time bar on the right side of the screen. This ill take you forward through time and show you what the satellite sees as it makes its way around the globe. Adjust the earth for best viewing angle.

Hook up your iPad to an external display for group viewing. If you have some 3D glasses (Anaglyph Red/Cyan), you can enjoy the visuals in 3D.[28]

Audience

Space enthusiasts, children, or anyone learning about the solar system.

Other Apps Worth Trying

- Star Walk: http://www.vitotechnology.com/star-walk.html. Android, iOS, separate versions for iPhone and iPad. By the same developer as Solar Walk. This app is about stars and constellations. Hold your device up toward the night sky and it will name the constellations and planets for you.

Classical Music History

Beethoven's 9th Symphony for iPad

- Developer: Touch Press, http://www.touchpress.com/titles/beethovens9thsymphony/

- Version: 1.1.1

- Platforms: iOS (iPad only), separate iPhone edition

- Price: Free sampler, with in-app purchase for full recordings: $13.99 for iPad (unlocks iPhone edition as well; for those who want the iPhone edition only, it's $7.99)

This app is a wonderful example of what an educational multimedia book can be. It's beautifully designed by Touch Press, well known for several award-winning apps.

The app is a deep exploration of Beethoven's 9th Symphony. The full version (go ahead and buy it; the free sampler doesn't have much content) contains four different recordings of the complete symphony: Fricsay, 1958; Karajan, 1962; Bernstein, 1979; and Gardiner, 1992.

A section called The Story is where you can read some of the history and context of this great work, with tips for getting the most from your listening experience. Sections include: A Brief History of Beethoven,

Beethoven's Ninth in Context, Listening to Beethoven's Ninth Symphony, and The Performances and Synchronized Score.

The synchronized score is one of the wonderful features of this book app. It works like this: select one of the four recordings and it will begin playing with the score moving along with the music on the bottom of the screen. You can choose from full score, curated score, or an image of the 1825 Royal Philharmonic Society manuscript (pages turn on their own as the music advances). The curated score is a nice feature, which dynamically shows and hides different instruments according to which are most actively playing. You can choose from large- or small-size notation (similar to increasing font size in text). There is also another kind of score (possibly for those who don't read music), which illustrates what each instrument is doing by a series of colored lines that move across the screen.

At any time you can switch between the four performances (continuing the music at the same spot), or move forward or back by dragging a well-designed progress bar with colored sections showing where the music changes. As you listen, you can read notes about what is happening, such as, "The key has changed to A minor, and the woodwinds chatter about it excitedly," or "The bassoon tries to remember the main theme, but we're in G minor now, and everything has changed." You can skip directly to each of the four movements by tapping in the top title bar and making your choice.

If you're wondering why the Gardiner performance from 1992 is at a lower pitch than the other three, a helpful note explains that it's a performance on period instruments and the orchestra is tuned slightly lower, reproducing the sound of orchestras in Beethoven's time.

As an added bonus, when you select the 1979 Bernstein performance there is a picture-in-picture video of the film that was made at the time, showing the players and Bernstein's conducting.

If all of that isn't enough, there is also an Insights section, which consists of about 90 minutes of short video interviews with experts discussing different aspects of the work. Included are Leonard Bernstein (from a 1979 interview), the well-known conductor Gustavo Dudamel (in Spanish with English subtitles), Simon Halsey (choral director), Suzy Klein (BBC broadcaster), Alice Sarah Ott (pianist, in Japanese with English subtitles), and several more musicians, conductors, composers, and journalists.

Audience

Great for those studying music history or appreciation, or for anyone who loves classical music and wants to learn more about this masterpiece of music history.

Children's Nonfiction

Bobo Explores Light

- Developer: Game Collage LLC, http://gamecollage.com/apps/bobo-explores-light/

- Version: 2.3

- Platforms: iOS (iPad only)

- Price: $4.99

The world of interactive books for children on the iPad is huge and could be the topic of a whole book. I'm including one here, because it's good for people of all ages to be aware of the reading experiences that children are growing up with. It will shape their expectations as high school and university students. So whether you work with children or not, I encourage you to explore this area. A great place to start is with this book app.

Bobo Explores Light is a delightful interactive book for kids (age 4–12) about the topic of light. Some of the topics included are lightning, fire, Thomas Edison, lasers, reflection, telescopes, color, bioluminescence, auroras, and photosynthesis. A cute robot named Bobo takes you on a tour through the chapters and leads you to text, photos, "fun facts," short videos, and interactive experiments. The sound effects are cute and funny without being annoying. The text is written in a fun and interesting way, and even adults can enjoy learning about these topics. Many pages have hidden features that you can discover by tapping on various elements (common in many interactive books for kids).

Watching the tutorial is optional but recommended, not only because it's useful, but because it's beautifully designed, cute, and funny. There is an option to turn on captions, and you can practice the interactive features. There are social features in the book—you can "like" it on Facebook and recommend the book by e-mail or via Twitter. There is a barrier to keep younger kids from doing this: it asks you some simple math questions to "prove" that you are an adult.

During your exploration of the book, you can skip to the table of contents anytime (tap on the small spiral). Move through the chapters by turning a gear wheel until you see the chapter you want under the magnifying glass. To see some beautiful short time-lapse videos, go to the chapter on auroras and visit "a swirling sky" and "fun facts." Other chapters have fun effects that you can discover by tapping on parts of the images (try the chapter on sunset-moon-sunrise).

Audience

Children ages 4–12, and adults who want to see the latest in interactive books for kids.

Example

The Morton Grove Public Library in Illinois recommends this app to their users along with other educational apps.[29] Libraries can be a good source of app recommendations for their users with guides like theirs.

Graphic Nonfiction

CIA: Operation AJAX: The Rise and Fall of Iranian Democracy

- Developer: Cognito Comics, http://www.cognitocomics.com/project -ajax.html
- Version: 3.0
- Platforms: iOS (separate versions for iPad or iPhone), coming soon on Kindle Fire
- Price: Free

The world of graphic novels and comic books (fiction and nonfiction) is experiencing some wonderful innovations when designed for tablets and smartphones. There are several comic-reading apps designed to read many different comics,[30] and there are also stand-alone comics published as individual apps (like this one).

Because it is published as an individual app and designed from the ground up for features of iOS, this app combines elements of film, comic book, and game to tell the true story of the CIA's plot to overthrow the government of Iran in 1953. In addition to the well-designed artwork of the graphic story, there are recently declassified documents, historic photos, and video film reels from the era, all viewable within the app.

The comic itself has 210 interactive pages, and there are 22 character dossiers with historic photos and notes. The experience of reading this book feels a bit like an animated film, except that you can control your movement throughout the pages. Subtle sound effects and music add to the atmosphere of the story. Typical sounds are seagulls, wind, laughing, a bomb exploding, footsteps, and gentle background music.

The artwork is layered and slightly animated in beautiful ways. When a character is introduced, you can tap on "roster" in the header of the page and a star indicates that the character has a file in the dossier section. Visiting that section brings up virtual file folders that contain historic photos and virtual type-written pages containing the person's biography. The feeling is that you are sitting in an archives and looking through file folders to do your research. You can easily return to where you left off in the book after reading these.

Creating an app like this takes years and involves a large production cast, similar to making a movie.[31] Cognito Comics is a developer to watch as they publish more interactive apps.

- Written by Mike de Seve
- Story editor Stephen Kinzer
- Adapted for comics by Mike de Seve and Jason McNamara
- Sound design by Andrew Scott Duncan
- Created by Daniel Burwen
- . . . and many more.

Audience

Anyone interested in the story of the CIA's involvement in Iran in the 1950s, or anyone who wants to experience the latest developments in interactive multi-touch comic design.

Other Apps Worth Trying

- Comics by comiXology: https://itunes.apple.com/us/app/comics/id303491945. Android, iOS (universal). One of the best general comic reader apps, with comics in many genres.
- Comic Zeal Comic Reader: https://itunes.apple.com/US/app/id363990983?mt=8. iOS (universal). Another good comic reader app.
- NARR8: http://narr8.me/. Android, iOS (universal). An interesting reader for motion comics and other interactive stories.

Short-Form Books

TED Books
- Developer: TED, http://www.ted.com/pages/tedbooks
- Version: 1.13
- Platforms: iOS (universal)
- Price: Free app; pay for individual titles ($1.99 each) or subscribe to all for $14.99/year

TED Books are short-form books that are shorter than a novel but longer than a magazine article. They are produced by TED Conferences and are designed to explain a single key idea in an exciting way. They are meant for those who want to be exposed to new ideas but don't have the time to read a whole book on these topics. They are available as only eBooks, not print.

The TED app is a reader for these books and includes multimedia content for each title, such as videos, photos, links to websites, map points, audio clips, profiles of people, and related facts. This additional content is brief and useful, and is designed in a way that keeps you within the flow of the book. Small symbols appear in the text to lead you to this extra content, and if you prefer to read without the extras, you can choose to hide them.

You may subscribe to the whole series for $14.99/year or buy individual titles for $1.99 each. At least 10 new books are published each year, and during your subscription you can read all of the previously released titles.

When you open the app, you are presented with a virtual bookshelf. Tap on a cover to see a short summary of the book, its author, and release date. Tap the "preview" button to read a sample, or tap the "price" button to purchase and download it.

The books are on topics such as education, the environment, brain research, or psychology. If you would like to purchase a title to experiment with, try *Beyond the Hole in the Wall* by Sugata Mitra. It's the story of an educator who experimented with installing a networked PC in a wall bordering an urban slum in New Delhi, and watched local children quickly teach themselves to use the computer. It's an inspiring story.

For each title, you may add comments and read the comments of others. There is a built-in dictionary, and you can adjust the font size, share a link to the book via e-mail, Facebook, or Twitter, and search within the book.

The technology behind this reader was licensed from Atavist,[32] which has its own app available, with different short-form content.

Audience
Anyone who enjoys inspiring nonfiction reading that can be finished within an hour or two.

Other Apps Worth Trying

- The Atavist: https://itunes.apple.com/us/app/the-atavist/id408059276? mt=8. Android, iOS (universal). More short-form content, similar to TED Books.

Made with iBooks Author

Calling Nature: Macro Photography and the iPhone by Bea Cantor
- Developer: Bea Cantor, https://itunes.apple.com/us/book/calling -nature/id590198557?mt=11
- Version: 1.1
- Platforms: iBooks (available on iPad and Mac)
- Price: Free

This book is just one example of an interactive eBook created with Apple's iBooks Author program. In this beautiful multitouch book, Bea Cantor shows us an exploration of macro photography using a special lens attachment for iPhones, called "Olloclip."[33] This lens attaches to your iPhone and offers three options: macro, fish-eye, or wide-angle lens. In this book she showcases her nature photography made with the macro lens. She gives tips for taking nature shots with this lens and includes photos of insects, flowers, mushrooms, and other beautiful items from the natural world. In the final chapter she includes ideas for doing school projects with this lens. She also recommends the Ollocip group on Flickr[34] as a place to see what others are doing with this lens.

The book includes still photos, slide shows, and short videos all taken with the macro lens on her iPhone. The slide shows and videos are a good example of interactive features that books made with iBooks Author can contain. Other books of this type may contain quizzes and 3D images.

Audience

Anyone interested in macro photography of nature. Good for teachers looking for ideas for school projects using iPhone photography.

Examples

The New York Public Library has used iBooks Author to create a series of interactive books from their collections. The series is called NYPL Point, http://www.nypl.org/point. These books include essays by experts, photos from historical collections, audio interviews, and more. Libraries could follow their example and make interactive books that provide context to their special collections.

See the chapter in this book, "Showcasing Special Collections," for more ideas and examples.

Other iBooks Author Books Worth Trying, Read in iBooks on iPad or Mac

- *Paperless* by David Sparks: http://macsparky.com/paperless/. Good book about going paperless, with embedded slide shows and movies demonstrating scanners and more. $9.99.

- *Frankenweenie*: *An Electrifying* Book by Disney Book Group: https://itunes.apple.com/us/book/frankenweenie-electrifying/id557041056?mt=11. Good example of an iBooks Author book with rotating 3D images (of the characters in the movie *Frankenweenie*). Free.

- *NYPL Point: Frankenstein, Making a Modern Monster* by New York Public Library: https://itunes.apple.com/us/book/nypl-point-frankenstein-making/id572663054?mt=11. Great example of how a library's special collections can be given context by turning them into interactive books. Contains articles, photo slide shows, audio, and more. Free.

- *NYPL Point: John Cage's Prepared Piano* by New York Public Library: https://itunes.apple.com/us/book/nypl-point-john-cages -prepared/id559342852?mt=11. Another good example from the New York Public Library. Learn about how the composer John Cage's prepared piano works, with embedded videos and more. Free.

Additional titles are available in the NYPL Point series: http://www.nypl.org/point.

Notes

1. http://www.amazon.com/gp/help/customer/display.html/? nodeId=200747550.
2. http://www.nypl.org/blog/2011/09/22/library-books-kindle.
3. http://academics.cehd.umn.edu/mobile/2012/01/26/ibooks-2/.
4. http://www.youtube.com/watch?v=f6-kEneezDk.
5. "MegaReader iPhone App Gives Access to Internet Archive's 1.8 Million Free Books in a Personalized Reader," http://blog.archive.org/2010/09/10/ megareader-iphone-app-gives-access-to-internet-archives-1-8-million-free -books-in-a-personalized-reader/.
6. https://archive.org/.
7. http://www.sppl.org/ebooks/cloud-library.
8. "Library of Congress Service Launches App to Bring Materials to Blind Readers." http://www.rollcall.com/news/library_of_congress_service_launches _app_to_bring_materials_to_blind-227849-1.html?pg=1.
9. Apple's page on braille displays for iOS: https://www.apple.com/accessibility/ ios/braille-display.html.
10. Find an NLS library: http://www.loc.gov/nls/find.html. Call 1-800-NLS -READ to apply for service (1-800-657-7323).
11. "Using Goodreader to Keep Journal Articles Organized, Aid Research," http://www.facultyfocus.com/articles/app-of-the-week/using-goodreader-to -keep-journal-articles-organized-aid-research/.
12. http://yalsa.ala.org/blog/2011/01/05/app-of-the-week-goodreader/.
13. To capture the iPad's screen, press the "home" button and "power" button simultaneously. You'll hear a clicking sound and the screen will be saved in your photo library.
14. "Recorded Books and Zinio Debuting Digital Magazine Newsstand for U.S. Libraries," http://www.thedigitalshift.com/2012/05/ebooks/recorded-books-and -zinio-debuting-digital-magazine-newsstand-for-u-s-libraries/. For more details, watch this video about how it works: http://vimeo.com/m/67167296.
15. http://www.imore.com/newsstand-vs-next-issue-vs-zinio-magazine -subscription-apps-ipad-shootout.
16. A list of publications available in Apple's Newsstand: https://itunes .apple.com/us/genre/ios-newsstand/id6021?mt=8.

17. This refers to the ability to purchase additional features within either a paid or free app. For example, games often are set up so you can buy more levels within the game for extra money.

18. https://itunes.apple.com/us/app/popular-mechanics-magazine/id393521916?mt=8.

19. http://www.imore.com/newsstand-vs-next-issue-vs-zinio-magazine-subscription-apps-ipad-shootout.

20. WorldCat's search API makes this possible: http://www.worldcat.org/wcpa/content/affiliate/default.jsp.

21. http://www.goodreads.com/blog/show/425-goodreads-grows-to-20-million-readers.

22. Goodreads librarians are members who have applied for and received librarian status on Goodreads; see http://www.goodreads.com/group/show/220-goodreads-librarians-group.

23. "Get to Know Goodreads," http://www.thedigitalshift.com/2013/01/k-12/social-medias-best-kept-secret-goodreads-is-a-fabulous-site-to-revolutionize-your-literary-life/.

24. http://apps4librarians.com/bookapps/.

25. http://apps4librarians.com/bookapps/resources.html.

26. FutureBook Best Reference App 2012 and other awards. See http://www.heuristicmedia.tv/press-contact.php.

27. http://www.amazon.com/London-Encyclopaedia-Christopher-Hibbert/dp/1405049251/.

28. You can make your own 3D glasses, see this video: https://www.youtube.com/watch?v=sIEn9z0oBE8. Or, order some free 3D glasses: http://www.rainbowsymphony.com/free-3d-glasses.html.

29. http://www.mgpl.org/kids/education-apps/.

30. Best Comic File Readers, AppAdvice: http://appadvice.com/appguides/show/comic-file-readers.

31. Watch a video of the full presentation from SXSW 2012 about the making of this book: "Reinventing the Graphic Novel for the iPad" at http://youtu.be/wP9p08LrZCo.

32. https://www.atavist.com/.

33. http://www.olloclip.com/.

34. https://www.flickr.com/groups/olloclip/.

CHAPTER 3

Apps for Productivity

Managing Files in the Cloud

Dropbox

- Developer: Dropbox Inc., https://www.dropbox.com/
- Version: 2.3.2
- Platforms: Android, iOS (universal)
- Price: Free for up to 2 GB of storage

Dropbox allows you to easily access your files from multiple devices. No need to drag around external drives; just sign up for an account and access your files from any of your devices, even while using a shared computer at a conference or in a hotel lobby. If you can access a web browser, you can access your files via Dropbox.

Do you want to collaborate with a colleague on a paper or use that photo you took with your iPhone on your office computer? Dropbox makes it all possible.

Sign up for a free account and receive 2 GB of storage. For increased space purchase a Pro account (prices start at $9.99/month for 100 GB).

Dropbox employs standard encryption methods to transfer and store data, keeping your personal data secure. Read more about Dropbox's security policy.[1] If you're at an organization that needs FERPA or HIPAA compliance, Dropbox currently doesn't offer that, so try Box[2] instead. Its features are very similar to Dropbox, with the added ability to support HIPAA and HITECH standards.[3] Many organizations have set up an in-house service using Box, such as this one at the University of Mississippi.[4]

Audience

Anyone who wants to easily share files between multiple computers and mobile devices.

Examples

- Teams who work in separate locations can easily set up a shared folder in Dropbox for documents they are sharing and editing.

- Dropbox is great for sending files that are too large for e-mail.[5]

Other Apps Worth Trying

It can be useful to have accounts on more than one cloud service, either to accumulate a lot of free storage space (they each offer some amount of space for free) or to keep different types of content in different places (perhaps you use Dropbox for personal files and Box for work files). They have all received good reviews and are worth trying.

- Box: https://www.box.com/. Android, iOS (universal). Similar to Dropbox, but with added HIPAA compliance (see above).

- Google Drive: http://support.google.com/a/bin/answer.py? hl=en&hlrm=es-419&hlrm=en&answer=2490103. Android, iOS (universal). Google's cloud-based storage.

- OneDrive: https://onedrive.live.com/about/en-us/download/. Android, iOS (universal). Similar to Dropbox, by Microsoft.

- SugarSync: http://www.sugarsync.com/products/sync_mobile.html. Android, iOS (universal). Another option, similar to Dropbox.

Managing Passwords Securely

1Password

- Developer: AgileBits Inc., https://agilebits.com/onepassword

- Version: 4.2.7

- Platforms: Android, iOS (universal)

- Price: $17.99

We all know it's not safe to use the same password on multiple sites—a security breach at one site can make them all vulnerable—but creating different, secure passwords of 15 characters or more is time consuming. Plus, remembering all of these passwords is nearly impossible.

1Password takes the hassle out of password management by generating secure passwords based on the requirements of the sites you visit. It then stores and fills in these secure passwords for each site, so you need to remember only one master password to unlock the app. Your passwords (and other information, such as secure notes) are stored in an encrypted file, accessible from all your computers and mobile devices. Browser extensions allow you to easily paste addresses, credit cards, and other information into websites. Your information is encrypted and secure. See "How Secure Is 1Password?"[6] for more details.

Audience

Anyone who uses multiple online accounts and needs to keep track of passwords securely.

Example

Imagine that yesterday you signed up for a new account on Amazon, using your home computer. With the 1Password extension installed in your web browser, you were easily able to generate a random password, something that looks like this: theV6tha5ty5fa. 1Password remembers the password for you, along with all your other unique passwords, and stores them in its encrypted database.

Now you are away from home, with only your mobile phone or tablet. Open the 1Password app, enter your "master password" (something you have previously assigned and is easy to remember), then find your unique password for Amazon and copy and paste it into Amazon when you are signing in (in either your mobile browser or Amazon app).

Now you have avoided the situation that often happens, where people use the same easy-to-remember password on multiple sites. When a site that you use gets hacked, only that site will be affected because you now have a different unique password for each site that you use.

And now you no longer need to remember multiple passwords, only the master password, used by 1Password.

Other Apps Worth Trying

- LastPass: https://lastpass.com/misc_download.php. Free for Android, iOS, and other platforms. Similar to 1Password. Premium version also available.

Creating To-Do Lists

Todo—To-Do & Task List

- Developer: Appigo Inc., http://www.appigo.com/todo/
- Version: 7.0.2
- Platforms: Android, iOS (universal)
- Price: $4.99

Todo is very useful for organizing your life with lists. It provides a balance between ease of use and multiple features, without being overwhelming. You can put items into categories and put categories into contexts such as home, work, or vacation. Todo allows you to integrate the Getting Things Done (GTD) methodology for task organization or use your own method. You can keep tasks synchronized across all your computers and mobile devices using Dropbox, iCloud,Todo Cloud 7,[7] or Toodledo (free web app).

Audience

Todo is useful for people of all ages who want to use lists to organize their life.

Example

MIT Libraries recommends Todo to their students in their guide "Apps for Academics: Mobile Websites and Apps."[8]

Other Apps Worth Trying

- Paperless: Lists + Checklists. http://crushapps.com/paperless/. iOS (universal). Another to-do list app, with a large number of built-in icons. You can assign a different icon to each of your lists for quick visual scan. It synchronizes across devices. Sometimes it's nice to use this for other types of lists than your main productivity app, lists such as groceries, gifts to buy, wish lists, ideas, etc.

- Wunderlist: https://www.wunderlist.com/. Android, iOS (universal). Another well-reviewed to-do list app.

- Clear: http://www.realmacsoftware.com/clear/. iOS (universal). See Koalcat's Clear for an Android copycat version at https://play.google.com/store/apps/details?id=com.xuchdeid.clear. Clear is another to-do list app, known for its simple, gesture-based user interface.

Managing Calendars

Fantastical 2 for iPhone

- Developer: Flexibits Inc., http://flexibits.com/fantastical-iphone
- Version: 2.0.7

- Platforms: iOS
- Price: $9.99 for iPhone, $14.99 for iPad

Fantastical has a beautiful and intuitive calendar interface that plugs into the calendars you already use and recognizes natural language. For example, entering "study break each Thursday at 7" adds the recurring appointment into your calendar on the proper days. DayTicker view provides a sleek, alternative way to see what's coming up in your schedule.

If your device supports dictation, you can speak the details of your event and it will turn into a calendar entry. Fantastical is a pleasure to use and a vast improvement over the standard calendar interfaces.

Audience
Anyone who appreciates clarity and simplicity of design will enjoy using Fantastical for managing calendars on their mobile devices.

Other Apps Worth Trying
- Calendars by Readdle: http://readdle.com/products/calendars/. iOS (universal). Another well-reviewed calendar app.

Accessing Your Desktop Remotely
LogMeIn
- Developer: LogMeIn Inc., https://secure.logmein.com/
- Version: 3.4.2511
- Platforms: Android, iOS (universal)
- Price: free with premium versions available

LogMeIn is a handy, free remote desktop app that works together with LogMeIn Free[9] for Mac or Windows. The setup process is easy, and once you have it on your computer and your mobile device, you can easily log in to your computer from anywhere. You can control your desktop as if you were sitting in front of it, zooming it to see the details and moving or editing files. It uses the same encryption technology used by online banks, for secure access. LogMeIn is free for up to 10 computers.

Audience
Anyone who needs to access their home or office computer from afar, over the Internet.

Imagine you are at work, but you left an important file on your home computer. Use LogMeIn on your mobile phone to access your home computer, and move that file sitting on your desktop into your Dropbox folder, which you do have access to on your mobile device. If you don't have Dropbox, you could use your home computer to send yourself an e-mail with the important file attached.

Other Apps Worth Trying

- Air Login: http://avatron.com/apps/air-login. iOS (universal). Control your Mac from an iPhone, iPad, or iPod Touch.

Printing Wirelessly from iOS Devices

Printer Pro for iPhone

- Developer: Readdle, http://readdle.com/products/printerpro_iphone/
- Version: 5.0.4
- Platforms: iOS
- Price: $4.99

Apple's AirPrint technology enables printing to many printers without installing any special drivers, so if you have a supported printer, you may not need Printer Pro. But it's very useful if your printer is not an AirPrint-enabled printer. See Apple's documentation, "Air Print Basics,"[10] for details.

Printer Pro allows you to print wirelessly to any printer attached to your Wi-Fi network. It also will print to any printer attached to your Mac or PC with a helper application installed on the desktop.

Audience

Anyone who wants to print directly from their iOS device who doesn't have an AirPrint-enabled printer.

Other Apps Worth Trying

- Cloud Print Plus: https://play.google.com/store/apps/details?id=com.pauloslf.cloudprint&hl=en. Android. Google's app for printing from the cloud.
- Print n Share: http://mobile.eurosmartz.com/products/printnshare.html. iOS (universal). Similar to Printer Pro, for using with printers not supported by AirPrint.

Accessories: Keyboards, Stands, Styluses

The following accessories are my top recommendations for use with the iPad. For excellent in-depth reviews of all kinds of accessories for mobile devices, see the website iLounge: http://www.ilounge.com/.

Keyboards and Cases

Apple Wireless Keyboard
http://www.ilounge.com/index.php/reviews/entry/apple-wireless-keyboard/.

The Bluetooth keyboard made by Apple is lightweight and works well with iPad and iPhone.

Adonit Writer Plus for iPad
http://www.ilounge.com/index.php/reviews/entry/adonit-writer-plus-for-ipad-3rd-gen/.

This keyboard/case combo gets excellent reviews because it can hold the iPad at different angles, has an internal rechargeable battery that lasts two weeks between charges, and works well as a protective case.

Logitech Bluetooth Easy-Switch Keyboard for Mac, iPad, and iPhone
http://www.ilounge.com/index.php/reviews/entry/logitech-bluetooth-easy-switch-keyboard-for-mac-ipad-iphone/.

Logitech is known for their innovative peripheral designs (mice, keyboards, etc.), and the "easy-switch" keyboard is getting excellent reviews. With a tap of a button, you can switch between three different Bluetooth devices (after pairing). It's thinner and easier to pack than Apple's keyboard, uses rechargeable batteries, and has backlighting.

Stands

Standzfree Floor Stand for iPad
http://www.standzout.com/View-All-Products_c_10.html.

Good solution for using your iPad hands-free while sitting in a chair or lying in bed. Great for musicians (read music on your iPad).

Styluses

A few of the best styluses available at the time of writing are mentioned below. See also this in-depth comparison review of many different styluses by Serenity Caldwell of MacWorld: "iPhone and iPad Styluses Compared." http://www.macworld.com/article/1164854/iphone_and_ipad_styluses_compared.html.

Adonit Jot Pro
http://www.ilounge.com/index.php/reviews/entry/adonit-jot-pro/.

This unique stylus uses a clear plastic disk as its tip, which allows you to see the fine point of the line you're drawing. This makes it feel more like writing with a smooth pen than most styluses. It has a screw-on cap to protect the plastic disk and is magnetic, so it can latch onto the side of most iPads.

Just Mobile AluPen Pro
http://www.ilounge.com/index.php/reviews/entry/just-mobile-alupen-pro/.

This well-designed accessory is both a stylus and a pen. Both the rubber stylus tip and the pen can be replaced. Comes with leather carrying case and a spare stylus tip.

Sensu Artist Brush and Stylus
http://www.sensubrush.com/.

A brush and stylus in one, for use with touch screen devices. It works particularly well with digital painting apps, such as ArtRage, Sketchbook Pro, Paper by Studio 53, and similar apps.

Pencil by FiftyThree
http://www.fiftythree.com/pencil.

A professional-level tool with a unique flat shape (like a carpenter's pencil) that comes in either walnut (wood) or graphite (brushed aluminum). The eraser tip allows you to erase without changing tools in the app. It connects via Bluetooth for many advanced features, such as palm rejection (it recognizes your palm and doesn't accidentally draw with it, so you can rest your hand on the screen while drawing). It's designed for use with their app, Paper (http://www.fiftythree.com/paper), and also works with other drawing apps.

Where to Find Reviews of the Best Accessories

iLounge (http://www.ilounge.com/) has in-depth reviews and ratings of accessories, such as cases, keyboards, stands, and speakers. Use their category search (http://www.ilounge.com/index.php/accessories/) to find reviews, sorted by rating or price.

Notes

1. https://www.dropbox.com/help/27/en.
2. https://app.box.com/.
3. https://support.box.com/hc/en-us/articles/200526618-Box-HIPAA-and -HITECH-Overview-and-FAQs.
4. http://technews.blog.olemiss.edu/2012/12/01/box-storage-and -collaboration-services-goes-live/.
5. http://blog.macademic.org/2013/07/04/sending-files-which-are-too-large -for-e-mail/.
6. http://help.agilebits.com/1Password3/security.html.
7. http://www.appigo.com/todo-cloud-collaborative-to-do-app-service.html.
8. http://libguides.mit.edu/apps.
9. https://secure.logmein.com/products/free/.
10. Apple's page about AirPrint: http://support.apple.com/kb/ht4356.

CHAPTER 4

Apps for Research and Reference

Dictionary

Merriam-Webster Dictionary

- Developer: Merriam-Webster Inc., http://www.merriam-webster.com/dictionary-apps/android-ipad-iphone-windows.htm

- Version: 2.1

- Platforms: Android, iOS

- Price: Free, Premium edition $3.99

It's handy to have a full dictionary and thesaurus on your mobile device (*Merriam Webster's Collegiate Thesaurus* is included with its dictionary app). It includes "Word of the Day," save your favorite words, and the ability to see a history of words you've looked up.

Another helpful feature, although available only when online, is voice search: speak your word into the app without knowing how to spell it, and it will recognize the word and look it up. Voice search is powered by Nuance, makers of Dragon NaturallySpeaking, which has been available for desktop computers for several years, so the technology is mature.

The free version is supported by ads, while the premium version includes more than 1,000 graphical illustrations and 20,000 additional entries covering people, places, and foreign terms.

Tip: tap the small speaker icon to hear the word pronounced.

Audience

This app makes sense for anyone who wants to have a dictionary handy without carrying a heavy printed book. It's especially useful for those who want to hear words pronounced aloud.

Example

You can speak to the app and hear words spoken within the app, which makes it easy to look up words within definitions. If you turn on the Voice-Over[1] feature of your Apple device, you can have the entire definition read aloud. For details, see "How to Make the Most of the Merriam-Webster Dictionary App,"[2] which discusses how useful it is for people with dyslexia.

Other Apps Worth Trying

- Wordbook (Universal) English Dictionary and Thesaurus:[3] Android, iOS (universal).
- Dictionary.com Dictionary & Thesaurus:[4] Android, iOS.

Wikipedia Client

Articles

- Developer: Sophiestication Software: http://sophiestication.com/articles/
- Version: 2.6.1
- Platforms: iOS (universal)
- Price: Free

Why use a Wikipedia client app instead of your mobile web browser? Lots of reasons! Articles includes a beautiful and intuitive interface, wraps text properly for your screen size, and has an orientation lock, which is handy for reading while reclined. Use the quick navigation table of contents and easily skip to relevant sections of an article. Search for words within a page, bookmark your favorite articles, and keep a history of your searches. Get a closer view of images and save them to your mobile device. You can also save articles you want to read later into a queue. It also uses the geolocation feature of your mobile device, enabling you to use the "nearby" feature to find Wikipedia articles about places near you.

Audience

Useful for those who use Wikipedia regularly. Travelers may use the "nearby" feature to find articles about places nearby. Students who are writing course-related Wikipedia articles[5] will find it handy for keeping lists of articles they have viewed.

Some libraries are contributing information to Wikipedia, by both creating original articles and editing existing ones. For example, the University of North Texas librarians contribute information about Texas history, with links to items in their collections. For more about librarians editing Wikipedia, see "Putting the Library in Wikipedia."[6]

Other Apps Worth Trying

- Wikibot 2—A Wikipedia Articles Reader:[7] iOS. Tabbed browsing, fully customizable font sizes, syncs browsing history, bookmarks, and reading queue with your other devices via iCloud.

Private Search Engine

DuckDuckGo Search & Stories

- Developer: DuckDuckGo, https://duckduckgo.com/app/
- Version: 5.0.1
- Platforms: Android, iOS
- Price: Free

DuckDuckGo is a unique search engine that protects your privacy by not tracking your searches.[8] Using it avoids the "filter bubble,"[9] a problem with other search engines, such as Google, where results are tailored based on your search and click history. If you're interested, you can read more about DuckDuckGo's philosophy.[10]

Use DuckDuckGo when you want to do a quick, private search and keep your information separate from Google's filtered search results. The app includes special search features, such as calculations, conversions, geography facts, music, etc.[11] It connects to Wolfram Alpha (described in this chapter) for its fact-based search results.

In June of 2014, Apple announced support for DuckDuckGo in the Safari web browser in iOS 8 and Mac OS X. This will make it easy to switch to this search engine for some searches or use it as your default for all searches. This is good news for the privacy-minded and will likely be available by the time you read this. [12]

Useful Features

- Save bookmarks within the app.
- Connect to Readability[13] for saving articles.
- E-mail or tweet links.

- Open results in Safari (useful if you have bookmarklets or other features in Safari that you want to use).

- A section called "stories" lets you browse and save news stories from their list of sources.

To learn more about the filter bubble effect, watch this video: "There Are No 'Regular Results' on Google Anymore," http://vimeo.com/51181384.

Audience

This is a good app to recommend to those who want to keep their searches private.

Specialized Search Engine

WolframAlpha

- Developer: Wolfram Alpha LLC, http://products.wolframalpha.com/iphone/

- Version: 1.5.1.47

- Platforms: Android, iOS (universal)

- Price: Free version, Premium $2.99

WolframAlpha uses a knowledge base of curated, structured data to provide direct answers to fact-based questions. Rather than returning a list of documents that might contain your answer, as traditional search engines do, WolframAlpha gives you some of the tools of a data scientist, making it easy to work with data.

WolframAlpha works best for those who need to quickly find fact-based answers. Topics covered include mathematics, statistics, physics, chemistry, engineering, astronomy, earth sciences, life sciences, units and measures, dates and times, weather, places and geography, people and history, culture and media, music, words and linguistics, sports and games, colors, shopping, health and medicine, and more.

Some highlights:

- Uses natural language input. For example, you can enter phrases like "What is the population of Los Angeles, CA?"

- Built on Wolfram's earlier product, Mathematica, so you can input mathematical equations and get answers.

- Includes hundreds of datasets, such as "all current and historical weather."

- Searches data from external sources, such as the FAA for flight paths.

- Integrates with Apple's Siri (and Iris for Android) to query when you ask a question.

- Includes: currency converter, stock analysis, almanac, and high-end graphing calculator.

The pro version launched in early 2012: For $4.95 per month ($2.95 for students), you can input your own data for analysis. It takes up to 60 different data formats, such as raw tabular data, images, XML, audio, and dozens of specialized formats.

Audience

WolframAlpha is very useful for anyone needing to quickly find facts and statistics. It could be a very useful tool at the reference desk. For search tips, see "Become a WolframAlpha Expert with These Useful Search Techniques."[14]

Examples

A musician can look up "C major 7th chord," and it shows the names of the notes, chord root, music notation, keyboard display, guitar chord voicings, intervals, and much more. Tap the "play" button next to the chord and hear what it sounds like.

Here are a few more examples of searches that work well with Wolfram Alpha:

"characters in a Midsummer Night's Dream"

"oscar for best actress 1958"

"harriet tubman"

compare things: "salary mathematician, physicist, chemist."

Unit Conversions

Convertible: Ultimate Unit Converter

- Developer: Efecto Pty Ltd., http://convertible.efecto.com/

- Version: 2.0

- Platforms: iOS (universal)

- Price: $1.99

Convertible makes it easy to convert many units of measurement and currency in a clean and intuitive interface. When you choose currency, a list of regions and countries displays and you can mark your favorites for easy access. It refreshes online with the latest currency conversion rates. You can share your conversions with e-mail, Twitter, and Facebook.

Along with traditional units of measurement, such as length, mass, currency, energy, and volume, it also includes playful nonstandard units such as snail speed, Judy Garland as length of measurement, bamboo growth speed, and more.

Audience

Convertible is a useful quick reference tool for anyone who needs to convert units. Recommend it to those who are traveling abroad and need a useful currency converter.

Example

In addition to the obvious uses, writers may find Convertible useful for generating clever analogies or comparisons using the playful nonstandard units mentioned above. For example, 1 grain of rice = 0.039 of 1 banana, and Judy Garland = 0.89 Alfred Hitchcock.

Other Apps Worth Trying

These are both worth trying, but not quite as fun and easy to use as Convertible 2.

- Convertbot—The Amazing Unit Converter: iOS. http://tapbots.com/software/convertbot/.

- Unit Converter Lite: Android. https://play.google.com/store/apps/details?id=name.udell.convertor.lite.

Mapping

Google Maps

- Developer: Google Inc., http://www.google.com/maps/about/

- Version: 2.2.0

- Platforms: Android, iOS (universal)

- Price: Free

Google Maps includes turn-by-turn navigation, built-in Google local search, public transit directions, street view, and more. Quickly search for local places by selecting restaurants, cafes, or gas stations.

Collaborative maps allow groups to create maps together. Build a custom map and share it, allowing others to add points and features to the map. For how to do this, see Google Maps for Educators[15] and the Google Maps Education page.[16]

Audience

People of all ages who need directions, are studying geography, or want to build collaborative maps of specific areas.

Examples

In addition to using Google Maps for directions, there are many interesting educational uses, such as creating a map of libraries or other organizations in your area, adding or editing places in your community, comparing neighborhoods, or using Street View to travel the world without leaving the room. For an example, see this map of all the public libraries in Vermont.[17]

Other Apps Worth Trying

- Apple Maps: http://www.apple.com/ios/maps/. iOS (universal). Apple Maps is recommended for those with vision problems because when you zoom in, the text labels stay large and readable, unlike Google Maps, where the text labels get smaller when you zoom.

Mapping in 3D

Google Earth

- Developer: Google Inc., http://www.google.com/intl/en/mobile/earth/
- Version: 7.1.1
- Platforms: Android, iOS (universal)
- Price: Free

Google Earth allows you to explore the world without leaving home. Fly to your location, search by voice, view layers of information including roads, borders, panoramic photos, and more. The interface makes use of intuitive, multitouch gestures, allowing you to pan, zoom, and tilt. The app also includes virtual tours and fly-through 3D re-creations of selected cities, such as San Francisco, Boston, and Rome.

See the Google Earth Outreach YouTube channel[18] for tutorials and examples of education and nonprofit use.

See also the Google Earth for Educators community.[19]

Audience

Google Earth is useful for people of all ages, especially those who are studying geography or who simply want to see visual views of interesting places around the world.

Examples

Glenn A. Richard, educational coordinator of the Mineral Physics Institute at Stony Brook University, has created "Teaching with Google Earth,"[20] a wonderful resource for using Google Earth in the geoscience classroom. It includes a list of useful ideas for classroom activities, such as an activity for exploring energy consumption rates around the world.[21]

Google Earth is not just for geography. Here is an interesting example. In an undergraduate English course where they were studying Virginia Woolf's *Mrs. Dalloway*, students were assigned to create online, interactive maps for characters in the novel, using Google Earth. They included pictures, sounds, videos, and the text itself in the map, which was then layered together to create a comprehensive map of the novel.[22]

Language Dictionaries

Languages

- Developer: Sonico GmbH, http://www.languagesapp.com/
- Version: 1.1
- Platforms: iOS
- Price: $2.99

Languages is an offline foreign-language dictionary app. Unlike many other translation apps, you don't need an Internet connection, since it downloads the dictionaries to your device. It includes the following dictionaries:

- Spanish-English
- German-English
- French-English
- Italian-English
- Dutch-English
- Portuguese-English
- Swedish-English
- French-Italian
- French-Spanish
- German-French
- German-Italian
- German-Spanish

Choose only the ones you are currently using to store on your mobile device; the rest are available to download anytime.

You may search or browse alphabetically. It also includes common phrases for most of the languages in the app. You can easily switch between the two languages in the dictionary, such as English-Spanish to Spanish-English.

Audience

This app is great for anyone studying a foreign language. And it's especially useful for those who won't always have a live Internet connection.

Other Apps Worth Trying

- WordReference Dictionary: http://www.wordreference.com/. Android, iOS (universal). Many languages available. Includes extensive lists of compound forms, voice recording of many words. Requires live Internet connection.

Language Learning

Duolingo—Learn Languages for Free

- Developer: Duolingo, http://www.duolingo.com/
- Version: 3.1
- Platforms: Android, iOS (universal)
- Price: Free

Duolingo's slogan is "free language education for the world." It uses techniques from gaming ("gamification")[23] to make learning fun. It includes English, German, French, Spanish, Portuguese, and Italian. It uses games and quizzes that rotate through different activities, such as transcribing spoken text, translating written text to English, identifying the English meaning of a word, or verbally translating some text on the screen by speaking into a microphone. There are placement tests to help you start at an appropriate level. You can compete against friends in the game and try to get the most points. It tracks your daily progress and can send you reminder e-mails. It's motivational and it makes language learning fun!

Audience

Anyone learning a new language and who enjoys games on their mobile device. It's a good supplement to traditional language study.

Other Apps Worth Trying

- Brainscape—Smart Flashcards: https://www.brainscape.com/. iOS (universal). Create your own and/or download premade flash cards for language learning and other topics. Uses "confidence-based" repetition, where questions you are less confident about come up more often in the deck.

Google Translate

- Developer: Google Inc., https://support.google.com/translate/answer/1075927?p=iosapp_about&hl=en&rd=1

- Version: 2.0.1

- Platforms: Android, iOS (universal)

- Price: Free

Google Translate supports more than 70 different languages. It's unique in that you can enter your query by speech or by handwriting for most languages. You can hear the translation spoken as well, by tapping on the little speaker icon. You can display your translation in full-screen mode for showing to someone (seeing it visually is useful)!

You need to be online while using it, but you can star your favorite translations for viewing when you are offline. You can also access your entire translation history when you're offline.

If you've used Google Translate on the web, you know that it's not 100 percent accurate. Some language instructors discourage its use. However, it's useful as a supplement to more formal training and dictionaries. It's great for communicating in a pinch when you are in a place where you barely know the language.

Audience
Language learners of all ages.

News Publications

NPR News

- Developer: NPR, http://www.npr.org/services/mobile/

- Version: 3.7

- Platforms: Android, iOS

- Price: Free

If you like to listen to radio shows from NPR, this app is for you. With it you can browse through individual stories, programs, or stations. Audio stories include written transcripts, and additional stories are available as written content only (without audio). If a story has audio, you can listen now or save to a playlist for listening later.

Another way to navigate is to browse the list of programs by title or topic (such as science, food, or books). Programs such as *Fresh Air, All Things Considered, Car Talk, Science Friday*, and *On the Media* are available. If you browse the "books" topic for example, you'll see a list of every episode from all of their recent shows that featured books and book reviews. Save your favorites to a playlist.

Browsing by station shows you a list of all NPR stations, by state. Tap the "locate" button and it will show you the stations nearest you. Alternatively, you can search for a station by zip code. Add any number of stations to your "favorites" list.

Audience

Those who like NPR shows and want to listen on the go. Especially useful for pulling out your favorite clips from many different shows to create a customized playlist that you can listen to while walking, exercising, or driving.

Other Apps Worth Trying

- NPR Music: http://www.npr.org/music/mobile/iphone-music.html. iOS (universal). Listen to music of all genres, read music news and reviews, listen to interviews and live streams of special events.

BBC News

- Developer: BBC Worldwide, http://www.bbc.co.uk/news/
- Version: 2.1.4
- Platforms: Android, iOS (universal)
- Price: Free

The BBC News app has many useful features. Listen to the live radio stream, or read the latest news from the BBC, with the ability to browse by region or category (technology, business, science, etc.). Set the font size from very small to very large with a slider bar, according to your preferences. Share stories by e-mail, Facebook, or Twitter.

Customize your app with the "edit" button, which allows you to remove sections you're not interested in and change the order of the sections on your screen.

You can also be a "citizen journalist" by tapping "send story" or "send photo." This opens up an e-mail to "talkingpoint@bbc.co.uk" where you can easily send your on-the-ground reporting to them.

This app also includes stories in Spanish, Portuguese, Chinese, Russian, Arabic, Persian, and Urdu.

Audience

Anyone who wants to keep up with the latest news from the BBC while on the go. Useful for those who want to read the news in various languages or contribute a story to the BBC.

Other Apps Worth Trying

Search the app stores for your favorite news publications. Try a search for your hometown newspaper, television station, or news from a place you will be visiting soon. Here are a few other useful news apps.

- AP Mobile: https://itunes.apple.com/us/app/ap-mobile/id284901416. Android, iOS (universal).

- Washington Post: https://itunes.apple.com/us/app/wash-post/id352 509417. Android, iOS.

- Democracy Now! War & Peace Report: https://itunes.apple.com/us/app/democracynow!/id331241955. Android, iOS.

Movie Listings

Movies by Flixster

- Developer: Flixter Inc., http://www.flixster.com/

- Version: 6.7.1

- Platforms: Android, iOS (universal)

- Price: Free

Flixster is an excellent app for deciding which movies to see. It's connected to Rotten Tomatoes (a site that aggregates movie reviews and tells you what percentage of the reviews were positive),[24] so you can choose to see a list of current movies sorted by their ratings. You can also sort movies by title or popularity.

You can find movies by browsing or by searching (by actor, director, or title). For each movie, see the ratings from Rotten Tomatoes, the actors, and the duration. You can play the trailer, get show times, and add your own ratings and reviews. Read the plot summary, see the rating (PG, R, etc.), genre, and release date, and see photos from the film. Read reviews from both critics and users.

You can also see a list of theaters near you (using your device's geolocation service), and you can mark your favorite theaters, so they always appear at the top of the list. Seeing nearby theaters is great when you are out of town and don't know which theaters are closest to you. When you select a theater, you can tap a button to phone them, tap the address to see it on a map and get directions, find nearby restaurants (linking to the Yelp app),[25] and see show times today or each day in the upcoming week.

You can also keep a list of movies you'd like to see, see all your previous ratings, keep a list of movies you own on DVD, and see the ratings and reviews of your friends (if you connect the app to Facebook).

If a movie is available on Netflix and you have a Netflix account, you can tap on the Netflix icon to add it to your queue. From there, you can also see and edit your entire queue. In the app settings, you can choose whether to show the ratings from Rotten Tomatoes or Flixster itself, and you can connect the app to your Netflix account.

Audience

Those who love movies and want to find the best movies to watch.

Movie Ratings and Metadata

IMDb Movies & TV

- Developer: IMDb, http://www.imdb.com/apps/?ref_=nb_app
- Version: 3.4.2
- Platforms: Android, iOS (universal)
- Price: Free

Having the famous Internet Movie Database available as a mobile app is very useful. In addition to the usual search for everything about a movie (director, writers, all cast and crew, awards, reviews, trivia, quotes, goofs, plot summaries, release date, languages, and more), you can view show times (turn on location awareness), purchase tickets via Fandango, and add your own ratings and reviews (sign up for a free account). The app will also keep a history of what you've viewed, make it easy to create and view a "watchlist," and easily allow you to e-mail show times, movie details, or a list of everything showing at a particular theater.

Audience

Movie trivia buffs and anyone looking for details about movies, directors, or actors will find this app useful. It's an easy way to find out what other films a particular actor was in or a list of all the movies by a particular director.

Examples

After you've seen a movie, pull out your mobile device and read the quotes and trivia sections to enhance your discussion of the movie with friends. Before going to the movies, use it to select a movie, based on its ratings and reviews. E-mail a list of movies to your moviegoing friends right from the app.

Specialized Reference

Chirp! Bird Song USA +

- Developer: iSpiny, http://www.spinysoft.co.uk/ispiny.html
- Version: 2.1.0
- Platforms: iOS (universal)
- Price: $3.99

This app is a wonderful way to learn the sounds of birds in the United States. It's based on information from the Macaulay Library at the Cornell Lab of Ornithology. The app will begin by setting itself to the region of the United States where you are currently located. Alternatively, you can go to the map and select a region of the continental United States, plus Alaska.

You'll see an alphabetical list of birds, with photos. Tap on the bird name to hear its call. You can sort the list of birds by first name, second name, bird group (doves, owls, swifts, etc.), song style (high pitched, long and tuneful, hoots and coos, and more), or commonness (from most to least common).

After you're learned some sounds, quiz yourself, using level 1 (10 birds), level 2 (25 birds), level 3 (50 birds), or make your own custom quiz. You can also set up an automatic slide show, including the birds of your choice, which cycles through your list, showing the photo while playing the bird-call. As an option, you can have it announce the name of the bird after it plays the sound. This feature could work well for blind or visually impaired users, because it doesn't rely on visuals, only sound.

Birdwatchers, students, or anyone who wants to learn bird calls in an enjoyable way.

Other Apps Worth Trying

- Chirp! Bird Song of Britain and Europe +: http://www.spinysoft.co.uk/Chirp.shtml. iOS.

- Chirp! Bird Songs Canada +: http://www.spinysoft.co.uk/Chirp.shtml. iOS (universal).

The Congressional Record

- Developer: The Library of Congress, http://www.loc.gov/apps/

- Version: 1.5

- Platforms: iOS (universal)

- Price: Free

Keep up with what Congress is doing by using this app. You can browse or search the Congressional Record from January 4, 1995, to the present. Copy texts, share documents by e-mail, and save documents to your favorite PDF reader. Search for specific terms inside each issue. To learn more about the Congressional Record, see About the Congressional Record.[26]

Audience

Anyone who wants to keep up with the latest proceedings of the U.S. Congress.

App Reviews

AppAdvice

- Developer: AppAdvice.com, http://appadvice.com/

- Version: 1.5

- Platforms: iOS (universal)

- Price: $1.99

AppAdvice is an iOS app based on the website AppAdvice.com. It's a great way to keep up with news and reviews of apps. Two of the best features are their App Guides and App Lists.

App Guides are lists of recommended apps in particular categories, such as Live Broadcasting Apps, Apps for Stargazing, Animation Apps for the iPad, and Best Calculators for the iPhone. Within each category, there are brief descriptions, the icon, and the price, organized by Essential, Notable, Decent, and Beyond. Select an app you're interested in and read a detailed review, with screenshots, a link to buy it in the App Store, and a link for sharing via e-mail, messaging, or Twitter. You can filter the list to see apps for just iPhone, just iPad, or both.

App Lists are similar, but they are published more frequently and often are themed for holidays or season, such as Apps for a Great New Year, Thanksgiving Planning & Turkey Apps, and iPad Apps for College. Within each list you can filter by paid or free apps. Other app lists are not seasonal, but are on specific topics, such as Great Reference Apps, Apps for Car Owners, Apps to Keep You Healthy, Apps for Movie Buffs, or Plan Events with Your iPad.

These guides and lists are a fun way to browse and continue to find new apps of quality. Other useful features include Price Changes (see apps on sale or apps gone free), and links to their podcast, App Advice Daily (a less-than five-minute video podcast).

Audience

Useful for anyone who wants to keep up with the latest apps in particular topic areas.

Examples

Librarians who want to keep up with the best apps in their field can check this app on a regular basis as a way to keep up. You may also want to follow AppAdvice on Twitter at https://twitter.com/appadvice or subscribe to their RSS feed at http://feeds.feedburner.com/AppAdvice.

Other Apps Worth Trying

- Best Android Apps: https://play.google.com/store/apps/details?id= com.androidtapp.best.android.apps&hl=en. Android.

- Appstart: https://itunes.apple.com/us/app/appstart-for-iphone/ id488613223?mt=8. Free iPhone app for browsing selected apps by category. iOS.

Subscription Databases

Publishers of subscription databases offered by libraries are starting to make mobile apps and mobile websites available. Unfortunately, many of these apps don't have simple, beautiful interface design like the best mobile apps do. That said, many of them have unique content and it can be useful to search these on mobile devices.

Some libraries are listing these apps in the context of their subject guides or guides to mobile apps. The MIT Libraries has a page in their guide "Apps for Academics" that lists these apps and mobile sites.[27] Since every library has access to different resources, I'm including only a few examples of subscription database apps in this book.

Because authentication can be tricky, libraries need to instruct users to be sure their mobile device is on the campus network or uses a VPN service to be seen as on the campus network (for apps that authenticate by IP address). Some apps need special instructions for setting up access, so libraries need to link to that information for each app where available.

Example

One library has come up with a creative solution for making their subscribed resources easily available to their community on mobile devices. This is the library at the Inter-American Development Bank (http://www.iadb.org/library). Many of their users are busy professionals working in different countries around the world.

Their solution involves a combination of responsive web design and a network authentication platform. If you visit their library from a tablet or smartphone, you see simply a list of the mobile publications they are offering as "apps." Their users simply log on using their username and password given to them by their institution and they can access each subscribed resource easily on their smartphone or tablet.[28] Solutions like these help users access specialized content easily and are greatly appreciated.

EBSCOhost

- Developer: EBSCO Publishing, http://support.ebsco.com/downloads/iphone_help/ehostapp/toc.html
- Version: 3.0
- Platforms: Android, iOS
- Price: Free app that works with paid library subscription

Search for and read journal and magazine articles on a variety of topics, including history, economics, and environmental science. E-mail saved articles. Save PDFs to cloud services, such as Dropbox or Box.

Libraries will need to provide instructions for their users on how to use the app with their institutional subscription.

Audience

Users who have access to a library that subscribes to EBSCOhost and who want to search journal articles on a variety of topics.

SpringerLink

- Developer: SpringerLink, http://link.springer.com/
- Version: 3.0.0
- Platforms: Android, iOS (universal)
- Price: Free app that works with paid library subscription

The mobile app makes it easy to search SpringerLink's huge collection of scientific documents. It includes personalized searching, advanced searching, and the ability to bookmark and save documents. You can also easily share document summaries with colleagues.

Libraries will need to provide instructions for their users on how to use the app with their institutional subscription.

Audience

Users who have access to a library that subscribes to SpringerLink and who want to search millions of scientific documents from journals, books, series, protocols, and reference works.

This app also allows unlimited access to SpringerLink's free content, including more than 127,000 open-access research articles, so it can be useful even for those without an institutional subscription.

AccessMyLibrary

- Developer: Gale, part of Cengage Learning, http://www.gale.com/apps
- Version: 2.1.2
- Platforms: Android, iOS (universal)
- Price: Free app that works with paid library subscription

This app includes information on health care, environment, biographies, career choices, literature, science, and more. It uses geolocation to find libraries within a 10-mile radius of where you are when you use it. You can also bookmark your home library so you can use its Gale resources when you are outside of a 10-mile radius.

When you find a PDF, you can download it and view it with the iBooks app or other PDF reader, such as GoodReader.

Audience

Users who have access to a library that subscribes to Gale and who want to search for information on the topics contained in Gale's database.

Other Apps Worth Trying

- AccessMyLibrary—School Edition: https://itunes.apple.com/us/app/accessmylibrary-school-edition/id371676736?mt=8. Android, iOS (universal).

- AccessMyLibraryCollege: https://itunes.apple.com/us/app/accessmylibrarycollege/id395238743?mt=8. Android, iOS (universal).

Finding Open-Access Articles

Some librarians are involved with searching for open-access journal articles to replace articles behind paywalls, especially when they are supporting MOOCs, with students from all over the world—many without a particular university affiliation. Here are a few recommended apps to help with searching for open-access scholarly articles.

- CORE Research Mobile: https://itunes.apple.com/gb/app/core-research-mobile/id523562663?mt=8 or https://play.google.com/store/apps/details?id=uk.ac.open.core.mobile. Android, iOS (universal). An app from the Open University for facilitating free access to scholarly publications.

- BrowZine: http://thirdiron.com/. Android, iOS (universal). Search, read, and save articles from open-access journals.

- arXiv: https://itunes.apple.com/us/app/arxiv/id302515757?mt=8. iOS. Browse and search the arXiv.org repository, hosted by Cornell University. More than half a million e-prints in physics, mathematics, computer science, quantitative biology, quantitative finance, and statistics.

- arXiv Mobile: https://play.google.com/store/apps/details?id=com.commonsware.android.arXiv. A similar app to ArXiv, for Android.

Notes

1. Apple's Voiceover: http://support.apple.com/kb/ht3598.
2. http://www.ncld.org/ld-insights/blogs/review-how-to-make-the-most-of-the-merriam-webster-dictionary-app.

3. https://itunes.apple.com/US/app/id289694924?mt=8&ign-mpt=uo%3D4.

4. https://itunes.apple.com/US/app/id308750436?mt=8&ign-mpt=uo%3D4.

5. "Why Wikipedia Does Belong in the Classroom": http://readwrite.com /2012/09/20/why-wikipedia-does-belong-in-the-classroom.

6. http://www.infotoday.com/online/sep08/Pressley_McCallum.shtml.

7. http://www.avocadohills.com.

8. http://donttrack.us/.

9. http://dontbubble.us/.

10. https://duckduckgo.com/about.

11. https://duckduckgo.com/whatsnew.

12. http://www.theverge.com/2014/6/2/5773480/apple-will-let-users-pick-duckduckgo-for-search-ios-8.

13. https://www.readability.com/.

14. http://www.makeuseof.com/tag/become-wolfram-alpha-expert/.

15. http://maps.google.com/help/maps/education/.

16. http://maps.google.com/help/maps/education/learn/.

17. Google map of public libraries in Vermont: http://j.mp/1j0JoUQ.

18. http://www.youtube.com/user/EarthOutreach.

19. http://sitescontent.google.com/google-earth-for-educators/.

20. http://serc.carleton.edu/NAGTWorkshops/teaching_methods/google_earth/.

21. http://serc.carleton.edu/sp/library/google_earth/examples.html.

22. http://chronicle.com/blogs/profhacker/mapping-novels/32528.

23. http://en.wikipedia.org/wiki/Gamification.

24. http://www.rottentomatoes.com/.

25. Yelp: https://itunes.apple.com/us/app/yelp/id284910350?mt=8. Android version also available.

26. http://thomas.loc.gov/home/cr_help.htm.

27. http://libguides.mit.edu/content.php?pid=174869&sid=1481866.

28. For more information on how this works, contact Sarah A. Berg, reference librarian in the Knowledge and Learning Sector of the IADB, at sberg@iadb.org.

CHAPTER 5

Apps for Taking Notes and Writing

Taking and Organizing Notes

Evernote

- Developer: Evernote, http://evernote.com/
- Version: 7.2.1
- Platforms: Android, iOS (universal)
- Price: Free, premium account available $4.99/month or $45/year

Evernote has many features that make it great for professional use. One of the most useful features is the ability to easily sync your notes between all your computing devices: desktop and mobile.

Not only can you access your information via the web, desktops, and many mobile platforms, but you can also input data in multiple ways, including by typing notes, taking photos, speaking voice memos, and e-mailing notes to your account.

The storage limits for accounts are not based on how much data you store, but on a monthly upload bandwidth. Theoretically, you can store terabytes of data as long as you spread out your uploads over time.

A unique feature: if you send an image, it scans and performs optical character recognition, so you can search the text inside your images. The recognition feature is not instantaneous; it can take anywhere from one minute to 24 hours to process. If you upgrade to a premium account, the images get processed more quickly.

Evernote includes browser extensions, so you can clip web pages (whole or parts) to save into your account. You can create notebooks to organize your notes, put notebooks inside of other notebooks, and set up shared notebooks for group projects (read-only for free accounts, editable for premium). You can also assign multiple tags to notes to increase search flexibility.

Evernote has a reminders feature, with in-app and optional e-mail alarms, and the ability to make to-do lists and pin certain notes to the top of each notebook.

The Premium account includes:

- Increased monthly upload allowance: Upload 1 GB of data per month to your Evernote account.

- Top-priority support: Get answers to your questions even faster.

- Editable shared notebooks: Allow others to edit the contents of your shared notebooks.

- Searchable attachments: When you add PDFs and Microsoft Office files as attachments to notes, you can search inside them.

- Note history: View previous versions of notes.

- Offline notebooks: Designate some or all of your notebooks for offline viewing.

- Passcode lock your notes on mobile devices.

Many other apps work together with Evernote, such as Drafts, IFTTT, Instapaper, JotNot Scanner Pro, Pocket, and Reeder. See the Evernote Trunk for more examples.[1]

Audience

Evernote is great for students, writers, researchers, and other professionals: anyone who needs to keep track of large amounts of information and access it from mobile devices.

Examples

Jennifer Carey, director of academic technology at the Ransom Everglades School in Miami, writes about using Evernote for research in history courses as a way for students to collect all their sources.[2]

Christopher Mayo has a collection of Evernote shared notebooks, showing the potential of using it in interesting ways.[3]

Kevin Eagan, on the blog *Critical Margins*, writes about scanning handwritten notes to save in Evernote. The app can then recognize and save the words in your image—if your handwriting is clear enough![4]

Other Apps Worth Trying

- Microsoft OneNote: http://office.microsoft.com/en-us/onenote/. Android, iOS. Separate apps for iPhone and iPad, each free.

Handwriting and Drawing

Penultimate

- Developer: Evernote, http://evernote.com/penultimate/

- Version: 5.0.2

- Platforms: iOS (iPad only)

- Price: Free

Sometimes the best way to input data into your device is through good, old-fashioned handwriting. Penultimate is the go-to app to fulfill this need, and you can use it with your finger or stylus.

Choose from different virtual paper backgrounds, including plain, lined, and graph paper. You can purchase other types of backgrounds, such as music notation staff paper, in their Paper Store.

Penultimate includes simple tools for drawing, and allows you to insert photos and draw on them. The lines it draws are very smooth, and you can adjust the pen size and save multiple notebooks. Send pages or notebooks by e-mail or to your device's camera roll, or open in other apps for different kinds of editing.

Since Evernote now owns this app, they have added handwriting features to the Android version of Evernote, instead of making an Android version of Penultimate.

Audience

Penultimate is great for anyone who prefers to handwrite notes and can be especially useful for architects, designers, composers of music, and math students.

Examples

Michael Andrew West of *Right Now in Tech* describes his use of Penultimate to help him become paperless in "How iPad Helped Me Become Paperless in College."[5]

Dr. Graham Basten, a teacher fellow at De Montfort University, describes using Penultimate to make live notes on his iPad connected to a projector during a biochemistry lecture. After the lecture, he saved the notes as a PDF document to add to class resources.[6]

Other Apps Worth Trying

- Paper by Fifty-Three: http://www.fiftythree.com/paper. iOS (iPad only).

- PenSupremacy: https://market.android.com/details?id=com.apking.ultipen. Android.

- Jot! Whiteboard: http://tabularasalabs.com/. iOS (iPad only).

Voice and Lecture Recording

iTalk Recorder

- Developer: Griffin Technology, https://store.griffintechnology.com/italk-premium

- Version: 4.6.7

- Platforms: iOS

- Price: Free, premium version $1.99

iTalk Recorder is simple: just hit the red button and you're recording. Record interviews, lectures, create high-quality field recordings, and share them through e-mail, Dropbox, and direct file sharing via iTunes.

iTalk Recorder is capable of multitasking—it can record in the background while you type. Recordings are in AIFF format in your choice of three sample rates (11.025, 22.05, or 44.10 kHz), and the app has the ability to append to existing recordings.

The ease of use and simplicity of the visual design makes iTalk Recorder a pleasure to use.

Audience

Anyone who wants a simple way to make audio recordings on their iPhone or iPad. Great for oral history interviews or lecture recording.

Examples

The University of New Hampshire recommends using iTalk Recorder to record lectures on the Disability Services for Students site. They also recommend many other useful apps for those with disabilities.[7]

The user experience department of the MIT Libraries[8] used iTalk Recorder for interviewing MIT students about how new technologies are impacting the way they work and study. Nicole led this study (Digital Scholarship at MIT),[9] which helped the MIT Libraries design better services for their students and faculty. See some of the results in this slide deck: Academic E-Reading: Themes from User Experience Studies.[10]

Other Apps Worth Trying

Both of the apps below integrate note taking with audio recording. Use them to take notes during a lecture, and during playback, jump straight to the part of the recording that was playing while you typed a specific note.

- Notability: http://www.gingerlabs.com/. iOS (universal).

- Pear Note: http://www.usefulfruit.com/pearnoteios/. iOS (universal).

Speech Recognition

Dragon Dictation

- Developer: Nuance Communications, http://www.nuancemobilelife.com/

- Version: 2.0.28

- Platforms: iOS (universal), Android version is called Dragon Mobile Assistant

- Price: Free

Dragon Dictation is based on Dragon NaturallySpeaking, a speech recognition technology developed by Nuance Communications. The app is easy to learn and use—tap the red button, talk into your device, and Dragon Dictation transcribes what you say. You can also speak punctuation—say "comma," and it will insert a comma. You can immediately see and edit the transcription. When done, you can send it as a text or e-mail, or save it to the clipboard. You can also use Dragon Dictation to speak your Facebook and Twitter updates, which is useful for users with disabilities, and for everyone. Many languages are included.

Audience

Users with disabilities that make typing difficult, and anyone who wants to take advantage of the ease of speaking to their device instead of typing.

Example

The Yale Center for Dyslexia & Creativity recommends Dragon NaturallySpeaking (desktop versions) for students who have word-retrieval difficulties, graphomotor weaknesses, or problems committing ideas to paper in a timely fashion.[11]

Now that it's also an app, many schools recommend it as one of the best apps to get for your iPad.

Other Apps Worth Trying

- Dragon Mobile Assistant: https://play.google.com/store/apps/details?id=com.nuance.balerion. Android.

Scanning

JotNot Pro

- Developer: MobiTech 3000, http://www.mobitech3000.com/applications.html
- Version: 4.2.0
- Platforms: iOS (universal)
- Price: $2.99, free version also available called JotNot Scanner

JotNot Pro is a document scanner in your pocket. Use the camera in your mobile device to photograph articles, documents, receipts, and more, and JotNot Pro will save a clear copy.

You can flatten out document wrinkles after scanning using JotNot's image-processing tools, which include image stabilization, white balance, and edge detection. Scan multiple pages into one document and save in different formats, including PDF or JPEG; e-mail your scans; connect to Dropbox, Evernote, Google Drive, and other cloud services.

It's nice to have all your scans in one list, but even better to store in a cloud service, which is easily done. You could even save your scans to GoodReader and annotate your documents.

Audience

JotNot Pro is handy for anyone who wants to scan receipts and e-mail them, or anyone who wants to scan and save a few pages of a book or journal.

Examples

In "Going Paperless with Your iPhone and Evernote," Thanh Pham describes a step-by-step process for scanning documents and storing them in Evernote. He uses JotNot Scanner.[12]

In addition to the uses you can imagine by having a scanner in your pocket, music students can capture scores they want to study.[13]

Other Apps Worth Trying

- TurboScan: http://turboscanapp.com/. Android, iOS.
- Genius Scan: http://www.thegrizzlylabs.com/genius-scan/. Android, iOS (universal).

Designing Posters, Newsletters, Reports, and Editing Microsoft Office Documents

Pages

- Developer: Apple Inc., http://www.apple.com/ios/pages/
- Version: 2
- Platforms: iOS (universal)
- Price: $9.99 (free on new iOS devices)

Apple's Pages is part of their iWork suite, which also includes Numbers[14] (spreadsheets) and Keynote[15] (presentations). It runs on both Mac OS X and iOS, and allows you to create beautiful letters, reports, flyers, and other documents. It's easy to share documents in multiple ways: e-mail, print, copy to iTunes, open in other apps, and access your files on any device using iCloud.

You can easily share with others who are using Microsoft Office[16] on a Mac or PC. Just save as a Word, Excel, or PowerPoint file.

As of September 2013, Pages and the other iWork apps come free with new iOS devices.

Audience

Anyone who would like an easy way to create beautiful documents, such as posters, flyers, or newsletters.

Other Apps Worth Trying

- Documents to Go Standard: http://www.dataviz.com/products/documentstogo/iphone/. Android, iOS (universal). Android version is called Docs to Go.

- Google Docs: https://www.google.com/mobile/drive/#docs. Android, iOS (universal).

- Google Sheets: http://www.google.com/sheets/about/. Android, iOS (universal).

- Google Slides: http://www.google.com/slides/about/. Android, with iOS coming soon.

- Microsoft Word for iPad: https://itunes.apple.com/us/app/microsoft-word-for-ipad/id586447913?mt=8. iPad. The app is free, but to create and edit documents, you'll need an Office 365 subscription: http://office.microsoft.com/.[17]

- Microsoft Excel for iPad: https://itunes.apple.com/us/app/microsoft-excel-for-ipad/id586683407?mt=8. The app is free, but to create and edit documents, you'll need an Office 365 subscription: http://office.microsoft.com/.

- Microsoft PowerPoint for iPad: https://itunes.apple.com/us/app/microsoft-powerpoint-for-ipad/id586449534?mt=8. The app is free, but to create and edit documents, you'll need an Office 365 subscription: http://office.microsoft.com/.

- Cloud On: http://www.cloudon.com/. Uses a back-end virtual server connection to present real Microsoft Office apps on your mobile device. Android, iOS (universal).

- hopTo: http://hopto.com/. iOS (iPad only).

Managing Citations and Bibliographies

Papers 3 for iOS

- Developer: Mekentosj, http://papersapp.com/ios/
- Version: 3.1.1
- Platforms: iOS (universal)
- Price: $9.99

Papers has a user-friendly interface for organizing and annotating your PDF articles. You can drag PDFs into your library (in the desktop version), and it looks for matching copies in online repositories in order to include relevant metadata (author, journal title, etc.).

You can also search within the app and download papers from there. It works with several library databases, such as PubMed, IEEE Explore, and Web of Science. It also searches Google Scholar.

You can sync your library across devices if you are on the same Wi-Fi network. Full-screen reading mode is conducive to focusing on one article. You can group your papers into collections, and make smart collections based on metadata for each, similar to smart playlists in iTunes. You can highlight text (with different colors) and add notes.

The "Magic Manuscript" feature in the desktop app (available for Mac or Windows) makes it easy to insert citations into your writing. It's also simple to click "insert bibliography," and then format the citations in the style you need from the long list of built-in styles. Many tutorials[18] are available to help with every aspect of using this app.

You can also export your Papers library to other citation managers, such as EndNote (via EndNote XML format), RefWorks, Zotero (via RIS format), or BibTeX, and use one of those products to insert citations into your paper.

For more information about choosing a citation management tool, see this useful guide from the MIT Libraries: "Useful Citation Management Tools."[19]

Audience

This app is useful for students and others who need to organize their research and format bibliographies in particular citation styles.

Other Apps Worth Trying

Here are three other popular citation management apps.

- EasyBib: https://itunes.apple.com/us/app/easybib/id436768184?mt=8. Android, iOS.

- Mendeley: https://itunes.apple.com/en/app/mendeley-reference -manager/id380669300?mt=8. iOS (universal). For Android, see Scholarly: https://play.google.com/store/apps/details?id=info.matthew wardrop.scholarley&hl=en (an unofficial Mendeley app).

- ZotPad: http://www.zotpad.com/. iOS (universal). An app for Zotero.

Mind Mapping

MindMeister

- Developer: MeisterLabs, http://www.mindmeister.com/mobile
- Version: 5.3.4
- Platforms: Android, iOS (universal)
- Price: Free

Because it's so easy to learn and use, MindMeister is one of the best of the many mind mapping apps available. Set up a free account on their website, and make mind maps in your web browser or mobile device.

Create, view, and edit online or offline and sync later. Add images, colors, and icons. Organize your maps into folders.

Export your maps in several formats, such as MindManager, Freemind, RTF, PDF, and PNG.

Create up to three maps in the basic version, or upgrade to Pro, Personal, or Business for unlimited maps. MindMeister offers standard[20] and education pricing.[21]

Audience

People of all ages who like to use mind maps for visual brainstorming and organizing information.

Example

Emerging technologies librarian P. F. Anderson of the University of Michigan Health Science Libraries explains how she uses MindMeister for mentally organizing complex information and outlining what she wants to say in presentations. See her blog post:http://etechlib.word press.com/2013/01/22/bubble-blur-flip-spin-hoard-hug-part-two-now/.

Other Apps Worth Trying

- Popplet: https://itunes.apple.com/en/app/popplet/id374151636?mt=8. iOS (universal).

- iThoughts (mindmap): http://toketaware.com/. iOS (iPad only).

- Inkflow Visual Notebook: http://www.qrayon.com/home/inkflow/. iOS (universal).

- Idea Sketch: https://itunes.apple.com/ca/app/idea-sketch/ id367246522?mt=8. iOS (universal).

- iBrainstorm: https://itunes.apple.com/ca/app/ibrainstorm/ id382252825?mt=8. iOS (iPad only).

More Apps for Taking Notes and Writing

Here are a few more apps worth trying for taking notes, writing, or studying.

Text Expanders, Macros

Use these apps for auto-typing words and paragraphs.

- TextExpander: http://smilesoftware.com/TextExpander/touch/ index.html. iOS (universal).

- TypeIt4Me Touch: http://www.ettoresoftware.com/products/typeit 4metouch/. iOS (universal).

Browse the Web and Take Notes (Split Screen)

Sometimes it's useful to have two screens side by side: one displaying a website and the other for taking notes.

- Side by Side: https://itunes.apple.com/us/app/side-by-side-dropbox-support/id386528623?mt=8. iOS (iPad only).

- Taposé: http://tapose.com/. iOS (iPad only).

Concentration Aids

Use these apps when hearing background sound is better than silence for helping you concentrate.

- Coffitivity: http://coffitivity.com/. Android, iOS (universal). Ambient sounds for creative thinking.

- focus@will: https://www.focusatwill.com/. Android, iOS (universal). Neuroscience-based music service to help you focus.

Journaling

Use these apps for keeping a private or public journal.

- Day One: http://dayoneapp.com/. iOS (universal). Well-designed app for keeping a journal that includes photos and geotags. Optional alerts remind you to make an entry each day.

- Momento (Diary/Journal): http://www.momentoapp.com/. iOS. Keep a journal and automatically fill your journal with your social media feeds, such as your tweets, Instagram photos, and more.

- Moleskine Journal: http://www.moleskine.com/en/news/moleskine-apps-for-ios-android-and-windows-phone. Android, iOS (universal). Another well-designed journal app.

Notes

1. http://appcenter.evernote.com/.
2. http://indianajen.com/2013/02/28/using-evernote-for-research/.
3. A useful listing of Evernote shared notebooks: http://www.christopher-mayo.com/?p_467.
4. http://criticalmargins.com/2013/09/02/evernote-book-lovers-best-tool-sharing-taking-notes/.
5. http://www.rightnowintech.com/2012/11/how-ipad-helped-me-become-paperless-in.html.
6. http://isothiocyanates.blogspot.com/2011/01/using-ipad-to-deliver-biochemistry.html.
7. http://www.unh.edu/disabilityservices/ipod-ipad-and-android-apps-college-students.
8. http://libraries.mit.edu/.
9. The study proposal: https://wikis.mit.edu/confluence/display/LIBUX/Ethnographic+study+-+Digital+Scholarship+at+MIT. Results of the study (executive summary): http://libguides.mit.edu/loader.php?type=d&id=613063.
10. http://www.slideshare.net/nic221/academic-ereading-themes-from-user-experience-studies.
11. http://dyslexia.yale.edu/TECH_dragon.html.

12. http://www.asianefficiency.com/organization/going-paperless-with-your
-iphone-and-evernote/.

13. http://www.mactrast.com/2011/07/review-jotnot-scanner-pro-go-paperless
-by-turning-your-iphone-into-a-portable-scanner/.

14. http://www.apple.com/ios/numbers/.

15. http://www.apple.com/ios/keynote/.

16. http://www.apple.com/ios/pages/compatibility/.

17. Microsoft Office apps are coming soon for Android tablets and may be
available by the time you read this: http://venturebeat.com/2014/07/02/new
-microsoft-office-app-coming-to-android-tablets/.

18. Papers knowledge base: http://support.mekentosj.com/kb/getting-started
-with-papers-3-for-ios and tutorials: http://support.mekentosj.com/kb/tutorials.

19. http://libguides.mit.edu/citation-tools.

20. https://www.mindmeister.com/pricing.

21. http://www.mindmeister.com/education#pricing.

CHAPTER 6

Apps for Multimedia

Viewing and Studying Art

Art Envi Deluxe

- Developer: Open Door Networks Inc., http://we-envision.com/artenvideluxe
- Version: 3.6.1
- Platforms: iOS
- Price: $3.99

Art Envi Deluxe makes it easy to browse masterpieces of art. Its huge database of artworks is indexed by artist and by period (Gothic, Renaissance, Baroque, Romantic, Impressionist, and Modern) and contains information about each artist. A complete list of artists included is available on the developer's website.[1] In addition to Western art, it contains a collection of art by Japanese artists. You can save the images to your mobile device and use them as desktop wallpaper. You can also create slideshows with different transition effects between slides.

Zooming into images on your mobile device gives you access to details of each image that are sometimes difficult to see when browsing a printed art book.

Audience

Having all of this art in your pocket is great for anyone studying art history, or anyone who simply wants to enjoy art.

Example

The Mohawk College Library in Hamilton, Ontario, recommends another app in this series—Architect Envi Deluxe—in their well-designed guide to mobile apps.[2]

Other Apps Worth Trying

- Architect Envi Deluxe: http://we-envision.com/Page.asp?NavID=258. iOS. Similar to Art Envi Deluxe, but for architecture.

- Behance: https://itunes.apple.com/us/app/behance-network-creative -portfolios/id489667151?mt=8. Android, iOS (universal). Browse the portfolios of creative professionals in the fields of design, fashion, illustration, industrial design, architecture, photography, and more.

Virtual Museum Visits

MoMA

- Developer: MoMA, The Museum of Modern Art, http:// www.moma.org/explore/mobile/iphoneapp

- Version: 1.0.3

- Platforms: Android, iOS

- Price: Free

The MoMA app is a well-designed experience that can be used while visiting the museum or while sitting in your own living room, anywhere in the world. It has the usual information about the museum, including hours, schedule of events, exhibitions, and special programs. Links to ticketing, restaurants and cafes, the MoMA store, floor plans, and membership information are also included.

The best parts of the app are the audio tours and the images of art in the museum. To see the art, you can search for a particular artist, or you can browse the collection by artist name or by medium (drawings, film, paintings, and more). Within the medium, you can narrow by decade (such as paintings from the 1930s). When you tap on a particular work's thumbnail image, you can see an enlarged version that fills your screen. Tip: take a screen capture to use any work of art as your mobile phone's desktop wall paper.

The audio tours can be browsed by collection, by floor of the museum, or by number (if you are standing in front of a particular work in the museum, you'll see its number). Many of the works have special audio tours designed for kids. You can browse all of these in the "kids" section of the tours. The app also includes a special section called "visual descriptions" for those with visual impairments.

The "more . . ." section includes links to MoMA content on iTunes U, YouTube, and podcasts by MoMA (all worth a look). Many of these are recordings of special events and lectures that happened at the museum.

Audience

Adults and kids who want to visit the museum, or learn about modern art without visiting MoMA. Those with vision impairments can listen to audio descriptions of each work.

Example

The B. Davis Schwartz Memorial Library at Long Island University recommends the MoMA app on their guide to art apps.[3]

Other Apps Worth Trying

Many museums have apps; below are a few that are especially well designed.

- MoMA AB EX NY: http://www.moma.org/explore/mobile/abexnyapp. iOS (iPad only).

- Love Art: National Gallery, London: http://www.discoverpentimento.com/. iOS.

- Guggenheim Bilbao: http://www.tfinteractiva.com/. Android, iOS.

Drawing

Bamboo Paper—Notebook

- Developer: Wacom, http://bamboopaper.wacom.com/

- Version: 2.2

- Platforms: Android, iOS (iPad only)

- Price: Free, with in-app purchases for more features

Bamboo Paper is a beautiful, simple app for drawing, sketching, and taking notes by writing with your finger or a stylus. There are many apps that do this, but Bamboo Paper is recommended because of its simplicity. You create a notebook and begin to draw on the pages. You can pick from a few pen styles (each with three different widths) and from several colors. There is an eraser tool and an undo feature.

The colors with the highlighter pen are transparent, so when you place your finger down again in the same spot you are adding more color. This makes it easy to make beautiful drawings with transparent color and solid outlines.

You can import photos or screen shots into your pages and then make notes or draw on top of them. This is handy for annotating photos or screen shots in a visual way. You can zoom in for drawing details and then zoom back out to see the effect.

When you're done, you can share on Twitter, Tumblr, or Facebook. With the full version you can also export whole notebooks or individual pages (as JPEG or PDF) to Dropbox or Evernote.

In-app purchases allow you to purchase more notebook styles (and create up to 20 notebooks) and more pens (pencil, water brush, brush pen).

To see examples of what others have done with Bamboo Paper, visit the "Made with Paper" website: http://bamboopaper.wacom.com/made-with -paper/.

Audience

Anyone who wants to draw, sketch, or annotate on their iPad or Android tablet. Great for architects, artists, and anyone who works visually.

Example

Janet Reid, school librarian at Cold Spring School, writes about using Bamboo Paper on an iPad to give a demo to her students about the library catalog. She imported screen shots of the catalog into Bamboo Paper and then drew arrows, circles, and other annotations on them during her talk for students. The iPad was connected to a television for the live demo.[4]

Other Apps Worth Trying

- See Penultimate and other recommended handwriting and drawing apps in the chapter "Apps for Taking Notes and Writing."

Creating Art

Adobe Ideas

- Developer: Adobe, http://www.adobe.com/products/touchapps.html

- Version: 2.7.2

- Platforms: Android, iOS (universal)

- Price: Free

Adobe Ideas is a sketching and drawing app for creating vector illustrations. You can sync your drawings with Adobe Creative Cloud (2 GB space for free accounts) and then open them in Adobe Illustrator on your desktop or laptop. For an in-app purchase of $1.99 per month you can increase the storage space to 20 GB. It was designed to allow you to sketch your ideas on the go and later put the finishing touches on them on the desktop. This makes it great for professional artists and illustrators.

It has a wide variety of drawing tools (pencil, pen, paintbrush, marker), and includes built-in color themes and a color dropper tool to pick up and match colors from your photo or drawing. Stroke smoothing is a nice feature that smooths your lines and curves. You can choose to smooth while drawing (for more detail) or after drawing (for more smoothness). The app has up to 10 drawing layers and a photo layer for each sketch. You can duplicate layers, flip them horizontally or vertically, and smoothly pan around your canvas.

It's also useful for anyone who wants a fun tool for simple drawing and sketching. It can be used with your finger or with a stylus. You can import photos from your camera roll and draw over them. You can share your drawings on Facebook or Twitter, save them to your camera roll, or open them in other apps. It's a very versatile app that works as either a sophisticated illustration tool or a simple drawing app.

Audience

Professional artists, students, and anyone who enjoys drawing on their iPad.

Examples

Scan a page from a coloring book (geometric designs are fun) and import as a photo layer. Then use the colors and drawing tools to fill it in (using different amounts of transparency). Zooming in allows you to see the details and fill in tiny spaces using your big fingers. This can be a fun and relaxing activity for people of all ages and skill levels.

Creating Comic Books

ComicBook!

- Developer: 3DTOPO, http://3dtopo.com/apps/comicbook/
- Version: 1.8.1
- Platforms: Android, iOS (universal)
- Price: $1.99

Comic Book is a fun app for creating comic strips from your own photos or artwork. Select a page layout, tap to fill each panel with a photo, then add speech bubbles, captions, stickers, titles, and special-effect filters to make a fun comic book page.

Save your pages as projects for finishing later. If you want more features, you can purchase additional sticker packs via in-app purchase. When you're done with your strip, you can save it to your device, or e-mail it as a JPEG or PDF. You can easily post your images to Facebook, Twitter, or Instagram.

This app is one of the easiest to learn of all the comic book creation apps.

Audience
Anyone old or young who wants to communicate visually using comic book formats.

Examples
Libraries could use this app to make engaging comic posters and flyers about upcoming events or to tell stories of previous events for library publications. Use it to illustrate a series of steps for instruction about library resources by importing screen shots and giving them captions.

Other Apps Worth Trying

There are many apps for comic book creation, and these are some of the best.

- Comic Life: http://plasq.com/products/comiclife/ios. iOS (universal).
- Halftone 2: http://www.juicybitssoftware.com/halftone2/. iOS (universal).
- Strip Designer: http://www.vividapps.com/Strip_Designer/. iOS (universal).

Making Photo Collages

Diptic
- Developer: Peak Systems, http://www.dipticapp.com/
- Version: 6.4
- Platforms: Android, iOS (universal)
- Price: $0.99

Diptic makes it easy to create photo collages. It's handy for illustrating a sequence of steps, or a photographic series, or simply for making fun and beautiful collages. Select from a wide variety of layouts, then add your photos to each section of the frame. You can adjust the frame dimensions with easy-to-use sliders, and adjust inner and outer frame thickness, shape, and color.

You can also add filters to each photo, change the color of the background, or select from many background patterns. Just about everything is adjustable, include the color hues, thickness and shape of borders, and fonts, sizes, and colors of the text you can add to images. In-app purchases are available for additional background textures and layouts.

Once your collage is ready, you can save it, e-mail it, or post it to Facebook, Flickr, Instagram, Twitter, or Tumblr, or open in any app that supports JPEGs. See the Diptic App group on Flickr for examples of what people have made with this app at http://www.flickr.com/groups/diptic/.

Audience

People of all ages who would like to create photo collages, especially those who want to illustrate a series of how-to steps or display their photos in interesting ways.

Examples

Libraries could use Diptic to make print or digital flyers illustrating a series of steps, showing a tour of the library, or any other creative use. See "Five Simple Tips to Make Great Diptics" for inspiration and ideas.[5] For an interesting article about how an artist uses Diptic, see "Portrayal—Missing Home by Jennifer Bracewell."[6]

Other Apps Worth Trying

There are many similar apps for putting photos in frames to make collages. In addition to Diptic, these are some of the best (well-designed, useful features).

- FrameMagic—Photo + Video: https://sites.google.com/site/mobilabios/. iOS (universal).

- Pic Stitch: http://www.bigblueclip.com/portfolio/pic-stitch. iOS (universal).

- Layout: http://www.juicybitssoftware.com/layout/. iOS (universal).

Specialized Camera Tool

Pro HDR

- Developer: eyeApps LLC, http://www.eyeapps.com/
- Version: 4.5.1

- Platforms: Android, iOS (universal)
- Price: $1.99

Pro HDR is an app that takes a dark exposure and a light exposure and blends them together for a beautiful photo that gives you better detail in photos with shadows and highlights.

iPhones have a built-in HDR feature, but Pro HDR gives you more adjustments and better control over the images. After you tap the camera button in the app, you need to hold your phone very still (or use a tripod) while it analyzes the light and dark and then snaps the two photos. When it's ready the phone vibrates and brings you to a screen with a preview image and adjustment sliders for brightness, contrast, saturation, warmth, and tint. Make any adjustments you like and after each, tap "save" to save it to your camera roll.

If you like, you can also crop the photo, browse through a collection of filters to apply (similar to Instagram), or select a frame from a collection of different styles. You can also add some text on top of the image, if you like.

The wonderful thing about this app is that it enables you to take beautiful images in situations where there is usually too much shadow or highlight to see all the detail of the image.

Audience
Anyone who enjoys mobile photography and wants to create better images.

Other Apps Worth Trying
- True HDR: http://www.pictional.com/TrueHDR/Overview.html. iOS (universal). Another well-designed HDR app.
- Photosynth: http://photosynth.net/. iOS. Microsoft's app for making unique panoramic and 3D photos.

Editing Photos

Adobe Photoshop Express
- Developer: Adobe, http://www.adoberevel.com/apps/photoshopexpress
- Version: 4.5.1
- Platforms: Android, iOS (universal)
- Price: Free

Adobe Photoshop Express is a powerful mobile app for touching up and editing photos on your mobile device. It's easy to use and learn. It allows you to crop, straighten, rotate and flip your photos, and remove red eye. There are several filters for changing the appearance of your photo or creating artistic effects. You can also add borders and frames, choosing from several styles. In-app purchases are available for more filters and for noise reduction.

Since this app is from Adobe, it includes the ability to upload photos to their own photo-sharing site called Adobe Revel.[7] It's designed to make it easy for families and groups to privately share photos with each other.

Additional options make it easy to share your photos on Facebook, Twitter, Flickr, Tumblr, or by e-mail.

Audience
Anyone who wants to edit their photos on their mobile device.

Other Apps Worth Trying

There are many photo-editing apps. These three are especially well designed.

- Photo Editor by Aviary: http://aviary.com/. Android, iOS (universal).
- Photogene 4: http://www.mobile-pond.com/mobile-pond/products.html. iOS (universal).
- Snapseed: https://support.google.com/snapseed/. Android, iOS (universal).

Identifying Music

SoundHound

- Developer: SoundHound Inc., http://www.soundhound.com/
- Version: 5.6
- Platforms: Android, iOS (universal)
- Price: Free

Have you ever heard some music playing and wished you knew what it was? If so, SoundHound is for you. Just open the app, tap the large button, and wait a few seconds while SoundHound listens to the music. When it's done it will show you the song name, artist, and album cover, if available. Of course, once in a while it can't find a song because it's not in their database. But usually it works.

Once you have identified the song, you can tap a button to hear a short sample of the song, follow links to YouTube videos for the song, listen for free in Spotify or iTunes Radio, or launch a Pandora[8] station based on the song. If you want to purchase the song on iTunes, there is a direct link for that. SoundHound keeps a list of every song you've searched for in your history, and you can also create a list of favorites by bookmarking individual songs.

Another unique feature of SoundHound is that it can (usually) identify songs that you sing, hum, or whistle into the app. Just tap the button and give it a try. You need to hum for only about 10 seconds. If you'd like to test it, try humming or singing the beginning of "Somewhere Over the Rainbow." You'll notice that it finds versions by many different artists and you can select the one you like.

Many songs also have lyrics available that are displayed within the app. If copyright doesn't allow that, it will show a "look up lyrics" link that takes you to a Google search for the lyrics. You can also easily share songs on Facebook, Twitter, or e-mail from within the app.

Audience
Music lovers and anyone who wants to identify songs.

Other Apps Worth Trying

- Shazam: http://www.shazam.com/. Android, iOS (universal). Shazam does the same thing as SoundHound. It's worth having both apps because sometimes a song will be found in one app but not the other, since they use different databases of music.

Listening to Radio Stations Worldwide

TuneIn Radio Pro

- Developer: TuneIn, http://tunein.com/get-tunein/
- Version: 5.0.1
- Platforms: Android, iOS (universal)
- Price: $3.99 (free version available with fewer features)

If you enjoy listening to radio stations and podcasts from around the world, TuneIn Radio is the app to use. With it you can choose from more than 100,000 radio stations and 2 million podcasts for streaming to your mobile device.

The variety of ways you can browse make it especially useful. Tap the browse icon, then tap "local radio," and your app will find all nearby stations. This is handy when you're traveling and would like to hear local radio from your new location—or quickly find your favorite local stations at home. You can also browse by genre: music, sports, news, or talk radio. Within each of those, browse more specifically—music categories include blues, classical, college radio, folk, hip hop, indie rock, jazz, salsa, and many more. Mark stations as favorites and then quickly access them in your list, which you can sort in any way you like.

If you tap the "live" button, you are presented with a list of categories, such as Celtic Music, Entrepreneurship, Film, or Technology. Be sure to tap the "edit" button to customize your list of interests. Then TuneIn will show you random stations that are live right now in each of your selected topics. This helps you find interesting new stations you might not know about.

In addition to radio stations, you can find specific shows and podcasts, such as *Morning Edition, Democracy Now, BBC Newshour*, and more. No matter how specific your interests, you can find a station or show in TuneIn to listen to.

When you are on a specific station, you can view the playlist of upcoming selections, set alarms or sleep timer, or share your current station on Facebook, Twittle, Google+, or by e-mail.

One of the best features of the Pro edition (worth paying for) is the ability to record live radio. At any time you can tap the red "record" button and it will record the current station and save to your device until you hit "stop." (Set a preference to control the maximum recording length.) Even better is the ability to set up a timed recording. Do you know of a live concert or event coming up? Select your station and set the start and end times and it will record and save to your device.

In the settings section you can select "car mode" to see large buttons, easy to tap while your device is mounted in your car and connected to your car radio. Set up a free account to save your favorites and preferences so you can access them on multiple devices. On desktop computers, access your account via the web at http://tunein.com/.

Audience

Anyone who enjoys listening to music, news, sports, or talk and wants to easily access shows from around the world. Great for foreign-language learners (get stations in your target language), visually impaired people (it's all about the audio), and travelers who want to hear stations from new locations or from back at home.

Other Apps Worth Trying

■ See the chapter "Listening to Audio and Video Podcasts.

Listening to Streaming Music

Pandora Radio

■ Developer: Pandora Media Inc., http://www.pandora.com/

■ Version: 5.1

■ Platforms: Android, iOS (universal)

■ Price: Free; upgrade to Pandora One for $36/year

Pandora Radio is a service for creating "stations" that play music you love. To create a station, enter the name of an artist or particular song that you like and it finds music that is similar to it and cycles through those tracks. It's a nice way to find music you might not have heard of but that you would like. Their system includes many new and independent artists and labels, and since it categorizes each track by the qualities of the music, it gives new and lesser-known artists equal footing with those that are well known.

Their system is not based on finding songs similar to what people who like a song also like; instead it uses metadata from the Music Genome Project.[9] This is a system where trained music analysts (musicologists, musicians, people with PhDs in music) assign tags based on up to 450 characteristics. These characteristics include everything from instrumentation, to rhythm, to key, and more. For example, tags might be: major key tonality, melodic songwriting, and a dynamic male vocalist.

While a station is playing, you can tap icons for "thumbs up" or "thumbs down" and it will play more music with similar qualities to those you liked and fewer songs similar to those you don't like. For each station, you can add more music based on a particular song you like. You can also add particular songs to your bookmarks list. There are links to purchase a song on iTunes, or to share a station or track on Facebook, Twitter, or e-mail.

You can wake up or fall asleep to music with the sleep timer or alarm clock. If you want to see what your friends are listening to (or share your own listening), you can connect it to your Facebook account.

If you want to get rid of ads, you can upgrade to Pandora One for $36/year or $3.99/month. With this version you can also install a desktop app for Mac or Windows.

Pandora is expanding their service so that it's built-in on certain TVs and car audio systems.[10] You can also use Apple's Airplay technology or

Google's Chromecast to stream to your TV or audio system. Use a Bluetooth connection or audio cable to connect to any speaker in your car or home.

Audience
Anyone who loves music and wants to discover new artists.

Other Apps Worth Trying

- Spotify Music: https://www.spotify.com/. Android, iOS (universal). Another great streaming music service, with free and paid accounts. Has a very large database of music of more than 20 million songs.

- iTunes Radio: http://www.apple.com/itunes/itunes-radio/. iOS (universal). Apple's app for creating stations based on music you like—similar to Pandora.

Creating and Composing Music

GarageBand

- Developer: Apple, http://www.apple.com/ios/garageband/

- Version: 2.0

- Platforms: iOS (universal)

- Price: Free with in-app purchases for additional instruments and sounds

GarageBand for iPad or iPhone turns your mobile device into a set of virtual instruments (piano, organ, guitar, and drums) with a mobile recording studio. It's a simplified version of GarageBand for the Mac, but it's still packed with features. It's a great tool for musicians who already play instruments, and also easy enough for those who don't yet have musical training.

For musicians who understand the features, it's a good way to begin a project on a mobile device (brainstorm and record melodies, beats, and more) and then continue it on your desktop computer at home. It's also suitable for anyone who just wants to have fun making music on the iPad or iPhone.

Get started by selecting an instrument type, such as keyboard, drums, guitar amp, audio recorder (record your voice or any sound), sampler (record a sound, then play it with the onscreen keyboard), smart drums, smart strings, smart bass, smart keyboard, or smart guitar. Within each type, you can select specific instruments, (for example in keyboards, you can select grand piano, classic rock organ, electric marimba, and many more). The "smart instruments" make it easy to sound good by providing preset scales, chords, beats, or other features. It comes with many instruments and sounds, and you can also purchase a complete set via in-app purchase.

You can create a jam session with friends (over Wi-Fi or Bluetooth), or you can play on your own. Record multiple tracks, then save and share your creations. You can transfer songs/projects to your desktop Mac, so that you can continue to work in GarageBand there. Or you can e-mail them, and share on Facebook, YouTube, or SoundCloud. You can also keep your songs synchronized across all your devices using Apple's iCloud.

If you'd like to learn more about the details of creating music with GarageBand, this multi-touch eBook is recommended: *GarageBand for iPad—How It Works* by Edgar Rothermich.[11] It's available from Apple's iBooks store for reading on iPad or Mac.

Audience

Trained musicians and also those without musical training. Anyone who wants to experiment with making music, jam with friends, and use a mobile recording studio.

Creating Beautiful, Musical Sounds

Bloom HD

- Developer: Opal Ltd., http://www.generativemusic.com/bloom.html
- Version: 1.1.1
- Platforms: iOS (iPad only), Bloom for iPhone available as a separate app (also for $3.99)
- Price: $3.99

Bloom was created in 2008 by Brian Eno and Peter Chilvers. It's a generative music app, allowing you to create patterns and melodies by tapping the screen. You can set it to play on its own or to create your own patterns. The screen shows colorful dot patterns while the sounds play. Tap the small arrow and go to settings where you can choose from different "moods" (actually different sets of pitches), with names such as "neroli," "vetiver," "yang," or "tolu."

The resulting music is very calm with bell-like tones, creating an ambient atmosphere that could be used for studying in a cafe with headphones on or relaxing at home. There is even a built-in sleep-timer.

For fun, try using it with two people (each with their own device), each playing on a different speaker in the same room. The room will be filled with interesting, calming sounds.

Audience

People of all ages (including small children) who enjoy playing with ambient sounds.

Other Apps Worth Trying

- TonePad Pro: http://www.tonepadapp.com/. iOS. An excellent, fun app for creating music by tapping dots in a grid, making patterns that repeat at different pitches.

- NodeBeat: http://nodebeat.com/. Android, iOS. One of the best generative music apps for Android.

Playing Virtual Instruments

ThumbJam

- Developer: Sonosaurus, http://thumbjam.com/

- Version: 2.3

- Platforms: iOS (universal)

- Price: $8.99

ThumbJam is an amazing app for playing virtual musical instruments. It contains more than 30 high-quality instruments, sampled from the real world. ThumbJam makes it easy for both professional and novice musicians to play music in any style from rock, to jazz, to classical, to world music. The screen contains horizontal stripes that you touch or slide your fingers across to make music. It always sounds good because each instrument has built-in scales, so that no matter which stripes you touch, everything sounds harmonious.

There are a huge number of scales to choose from, taken from many world music traditions around the world. In addition to the Western scales (major, minor, major pentatonic, etc.), there are scales from Asian music (Balinese pentachord), European music (Gypsy hexatonic), Indian music (Devakriya), jazz (minor bebop), modal (dorian), and many more.

Some of the instruments included are: cello, violin, viola, electric guitar, electric bass, trumpet, trombone, flute, hammered dulcimer, mandolin, pipe organ, Theremin, several drum kits, tabla, ukulele, djembe, tenor sax, and there are many more.

Each virtual instrument is loaded with a default scale, such as harmonic minor for the pipe organ and mixolydian for the mandolin. To change the instrument, tap on the "sound" button; from there you can tap "change instrument," "change scale," "volume," "create instrument," or "download samples." Many of the instruments allow you to add vibrato by shaking your finger slightly. You can control the volume by tilting your device. This allows for very expressive music making.

In addition, the app allows you to record your own loops and then play another loop on top of your recording. To see this in action, take a look at the videos on the media page of ThumbJam's website.[12]

There are many more features to explore, so you can go in depth with this app, or you can just open it and start playing simply, without reading any instructions or learning all the features. This is a wonderful example of an app that takes advantage of the features of your mobile device and enables creative music making.

Audience

People of all ages who enjoy making music. Novices and professional musicians will enjoy this app.

Other Apps Worth Trying

- Balls: https://itunes.apple.com/us/app/balls/id303046432?mt=8&ls=1. iOS (universal). Fun music-making app where you bounce colorful balls around the screen. Go to settings to change the ball sounds, style, range, and more.

- Beatwave: https://itunes.apple.com/us/app/beatwave/id363718254?mt=8. iOS (universal). Create colorful patterns on a moving grid to make interesting music.

- Bebot: http://www.normalware.com/. iOS (universal). Drag your finger over a very cute robot synthesizer to create electronic music.

Playing Music with Others

Ocarina

- Developer: Smule, http://www.smule.com/apps#ocarina
- Version: 1.0.8
- Platforms: iOS
- Price: $0.99

Ocarina is a fun app for turning your mobile phone into an ocarina.[13] Blow gently into the microphone while resting your phone on both thumbs and ring fingers and holding down dots with your other fingers.

It takes a bit of practice to learn to use this app, but it's worth it, because the sounds it makes are beautiful and you can play in groups with others. You can tap the "world" button to see a virtual planet Earth and browse through the recordings of other Ocarina players around the world. To get started, it's recommended to watch the built-in tutorial for instructions.

Smule is an interesting company. Their stated mission is "to connect the world through music."[14] They aim to enable anyone to easily create and share music. Smule was founded by professor and inventor Ge Wang of Stanford University. They make a number of other music apps; see the list on their website.[15]

Watch this four-minute documentary video on YouTube to learn more: *The Music Man*, directed by Steve James at http://youtu.be/EVzP-FeTKfBI.

Audience

People of all ages and abilities who want to play music on their mobile phone.

Examples

Libraries could have fun events for teens and kids where people play music together, using apps like Ocarina. Provide a few iPod Touches filled with music apps like these and invite a local expert to give a training session.

Other Apps Worth Trying

These apps are similar to real-world instruments and are fun for both expert musicians and beginners.

- Guitar! by Smule: http://www.smule.com/apps. iOS (universal).
- Sing! Karaoke: http://www.smule.com/apps. Android, iOS (universal).
- Magic Piano by Smule: http://www.smule.com/apps. Android, iOS (universal).
- UkeMaster: http://www.ukulele.nl/ukemaster/. iOS. Tune your ukulele and learn chords.

Watching Videos

YouTube

- Developer: Google Inc., https://productforums.google.com/forum/#!categories/youtube/mobile-and-devices
- Version: 2.2.0
- Platforms: Android, iOS (universal)
- Price: Free

The YouTube app for iOS is especially nice on iPads. With it, you can access all the features of YouTube, and if you are logged in, you can see your favorites, likes, subscriptions, and uploaded videos. A scrollable sidebar offers links to all of these features as well as the categories for browsing. Tap on a video to watch it and you'll see it in a small window with the usual surrounding buttons for thumbs up, sharing on social media, adding to playlists, and more. You can also see suggested videos, add comments, and subscribe to channels.

If you return to the sidebar while watching a video (tap in small arrow in upper left), your video will keep playing in a small thumbnail window in the lower left while you browse or search for another video.

If you swipe out with two fingers on the video, you can make it fill the entire screen. From there, tap lightly anywhere and three small dots will upper in the upper left corner. Tap that to see three choices: quality, closed captions (if available), and flag. If the video is available in different sizes, you can select the size best for your situation (higher quality when you are on a fast connection). The closed captions are great for those with hearing problems, or if you want to watch a video without the sound on in a public place. They are also good if English is not your first language—it sometimes helps to see the words written out. This applies also if your video has multiple language captions—great for anyone learning another language.

The YouTube app for iOS offers a very nice user experience for watching videos on the go. With the large amount of educational content on YouTube, this becomes a useful tool for learning and enjoying recreationally.

Audience

Anyone who wants to watch videos on mobile devices.

Example

Many libraries create YouTube videos about their services and events. The YouTube app is a nice way to watch these and other educational videos on the go.

Other Apps Worth Trying

In addition to playing videos you have loaded to the device with the built-in video player (on iPads, it's called simply "Videos"), there are several good options for streaming video. The following are some of the best apps with a wide variety of high-quality content.

- Vimeo: https://vimeo.com/. Android, iOS (universal).

- Netflix: http://www.netflix.com/. Android, iOS (universal).

- TED: http://www.ted.com/. Android, iOS (universal).

- NFB Films (National Film Board of Canada): https://www.nfb.ca/apps/. Android, iOS.

- PBS, and PBS for iPad: http://www.pbs.org/digitalshop/apps/. Android, iOS.

- Smithsonian Channel: http://www.smithsonianchannel.com/sc/web/ways-to-watch. Android, iOS.

Streaming Videos from Your Computer to Your Mobile Device

Air Video

- Developer: InMethod s.r.o., http://www.inmethod.com/airvideo/

- Version: 2.4.16

- Platforms: iOS (universal)

- Price: $2.99

Air Video enables you to view videos from your home computer streamed live to your mobile device. To use it, you first need to install Air Video Server (free download)[16] on your Mac or Windows computer. Once the server is running, you select particular folders that contain videos you want to share.

Once that is set up, open Air Video on your iPhone or iPad and tap the "plus" button to add your server. After the server is added, you can easily browse the folders you have set up to find a video you want to view.

One of the best features is the ability to do live conversion of videos in formats that normally would not be viewable on iOS devices. As long as the video isn't protected with DRM (such as most videos purchased from the iTunes store), these formats will convert: mp4, m4v, mov, avi, wmv, asf, mpg, mpeg, mkv, 3gp, dmf, divx, and flv. You don't need to wait for the video to convert before watching it—just tap on "play with live conversion" and the video will begin streaming to your iPhone or iPad.

Optionally, you may use the app to convert your videos first and then load copies of them to your mobile devices for viewing in your regular "Videos" app when you are offline.

You can stream videos both inside and outside your home network. If your router doesn't support this, there are work-arounds described on Air Video's site.[17] It's a great way to watch movies from DVDs that you have copied to your home computer—you can do it while you're far away on a trip or while on the living room couch with your home computer in another room.

Audience
Anyone who wants to watch their own movies on a mobile device while traveling. Good for those who have good Internet connections but not much storage space on their mobile device.

Other Apps Worth Trying
- AirVid: https://play.google.com/store/apps/details?id=com.sb.airvid. Similar to Air Video but for Android.

Listening to Educational Lectures
iTunes U
- Developer: Apple, http://www.apple.com/support/itunes-u/
- Version: 1.4.1
- Platforms: iOS (universal)
- Price: Free

iTunes U delivers free educational content from universities and schools in 30 countries. Courses may include video or audio lectures, assignments, readings, presentations, and links to apps and iBooks textbooks.

The catalog is where you can browse or search for courses, and includes sections for universities and colleges, "beyond campus," and K–12. "Beyond campus" includes content from various organizations, such as museums, libraries, performance venues, national parks, educational television channels, radio stations, and more. You can also browse by category, such as business, engineering, art and architecture, literature, or language. It's also possible to browse by language, and many courses are available in languages other than English.

Courses have a "posts" section, which is the course outline, leading you step by step through the content and assignments in order. You can check off each unit as you complete it. You can also take notes within the app on the "notes" tab. Notes can be for the course as a whole or for specific audio/video or iBooks content within the course. The "materials" tab shows you a complete list of course materials, and indicates the format and whether you have downloaded it yet (for videos stored in the cloud).

The trick to using iTunes U is finding the best and most relevant content for your needs. Apple includes a section called "standout courses," which is a good starting point for finding the best-quality courses. Some courses are just a series of video lectures with no additional material or assignments. Sets of lectures can be valuable but aren't really full-fledged courses—they are more like podcasts. I find it helpful to think of iTunes U as a place to find interesting, free educational content rather than an interactive learning environment.

ITunes U may also be used on desktop computers, but it's very handy to have it on your iPad or iPhone so that you can view content on the go. In June 2014, Apple announced that it will be adding a course-creation tool within the app, and also student discussion forums. These features will likely be available by the time you read this.

Here are a few recommended courses, if you'd like to see examples of quality content.

Full courses:

- Cities by the Open University. https://itunes.apple.com/us/course/cities/id495058115.

- The Kennedy Half Century by the University of Virginia. https://itunes.apple.com/us/course/the-kennedy-half-century/id715737546.

Videos only:

- Justice with Michael Sandel by Harvard University. https://itunes.apple.com/us/itunes-u/justice-with-michael-sandel/id379064095?mt=10.

- Hidden Treasures at the Library of Congress by Library of Congress. https://itunes.apple.com/us/itunes-u/hidden-treasures-at-library/id391498646?mt=10.

If you would like some guidance on how to create a course for iTunes U, download this excellent course.

iTunes U: A Course Creation Guide for Educators by The Ohio State University.

https://itunes.apple.com/ua/course/itunes-u-course-creation-guide/id644450313.

Audience

Students and lifelong learners looking for free educational content from universities and K–12 schools around the world.

Examples

Libraries could create courses about special collections in iTunes U, such as Hidden Treasures at the Library of Congress mentioned above.

iPads in the library could be loaded with interesting educational content from iTunes U.

Other Apps Worth Trying

- TuneSpace: http://2kit.de/en/otw-portfolio/tunespace-itunes-u-android/. Android app for playing content from iTunes U.

- Khan Academy: https://itunes.apple.com/us/app/khan-academy/id469863705. iOS (universal) or KHAndroid: https://play.google.com/store/apps/details?id=org.khanacademy.videos&hl=en. Android. Khan Academy is a nonprofit with a huge amount of free educational content on video. https://www.khanacademy.org/about.

- Udemy: https://www.udemy.com/. Android, iOS (universal).

Listening to Audio and Video Podcasts

Podcasts

- Developer: Apple, http://www.apple.com/support/ios/podcasts/
- Version: 2.0
- Platforms: iOS (universal)
- Price: Free

Apple's Podcasts app is available as a free download from the app store and is a very good way to find, organize, and listen to your favorite podcasts. You can stream the episodes (which saves space on your device) or download episodes for listening when you are offline.

Tap on "featured" or "top charts" to begin your browsing of the podcasts section of the app store. Limit to audio podcasts, video podcasts, or search both together. Tap "categories" to see a list of topics such as arts, business, comedy, education, health, or technology. Tap the "subscribe" button for the shows you like.

Go to "My Podcasts" to see a list of your subscriptions. In the settings of each podcast you can make choices that determine how often to refresh (every hour, every six hours, every day, every week, manually), how many episodes to keep (all, all unplayed, most recent, last 2, last 3, last 5, last 10), turn auto-downloads on or off, and set the sort order and play order.

Tap the "i" button on an episode to read the show notes. Tap the cloud icon to download an episode immediately. You can create "on-the-go" playlists by adding individual episodes from different podcasts to your list. Tap on "my stations" to see your on-the-go list.

When you are listening to a podcast you adjust the speed to 0.5x, 1x, 1.5x, or 2x. There is also a sleep timer, a volume control, a pause button, and a skip button for the next or previous podcast. You can share an individual episode by text message, e-mail, Twitter, or Facebook.

Podcasts are available on many, many topics and are great for studying languages (*Coffee Break Spanish*), keeping up with technology news (*This Week in Google Glass*), watching cooking demos (*Vegan A Go-Go*), or keeping fit (*YogaJournal.com: Yoga Practice Podcast*).

If you have an Android device, try the excellent Pocket Casts app, listed below.

Audience

Anyone who would like to listen to or watch audio and video content by free subscription on their mobile devices.

Examples

Many libraries publish podcasts of their events and author readings, such as this one from the Seattle Public Library: http://www.spl.org/library-collection/podcasts/2013-podcasts. Put these podcasts on iPads for people to borrow or listen to in the library. Also, librarians could make guides to some of the best podcasts available in specific topic areas and make these available on library iPads. For another idea, libraries could host events for the public where people learn how to create their own podcasts.

Other Apps Worth Trying

The following apps are the best podcasting apps available, each with unique features worth exploring if you listen to a lot of podcasts.

- Instacast 4: http://vemedio.com/products/instacast. iOS (universal)

- Downcast: http://www.downcastapp.com/. iOS (universal)

- Pocket Casts: http://www.shiftyjelly.com/ios/pocketcasts. Android, iOS (universal)

- Stitcher Radio for Podcasts: http://www.stitcher.com/. Android, iOS (universal)

Editing Movies

iMovie

- Developer: Apple, http://www.apple.com/ios/imovie/

- Version: 2.0

- Platforms: iOS (universal)

- Price: $4.99, or free with purchase of a new iOS device

iMovie is a movie-editing and creation app. Browse the movies and photos you've taken on your iOS device and arrange them with interesting transitions and a soundtrack into a movie that you can share with anyone.

You can choose to create a movie (use a theme to get started) or a movie trailer (use built-in templates, such as superhero, retro, narrative, family, or scary). Select multiple movie clips or still photos and arrange them in a timeline. You can clip, adjust speed (slow motion is fun), select from different types of transitions, and then add audio. There are several choices for theme music and a set of built-in sound effects (alarm, applause, bark, car skid, police siren, thunder, and more). You can also add your own music or audio files from your iTunes library and record your own voice narration, if you like. Audio controls make it easy to trim, duplicate, split, or fade the music. An "undo" button makes it easy to cancel mistakes.

A simple option for getting started is to create a movie using only still photos. Select photos, arrange them, decide how long each will be shown, and iMovie will use the Ken Burns effect[18] to transition between them, panning and zooming in a way similar to what's used in his documentaries.

When your movie is ready you can share it in various ways. Save to your camera roll, send it in an e-mail or message, or publish directly to sites like Vimeo, YouTube, and Facebook. You can also wirelessly stream your movies to an HDTV with Apple TV.

The gesture-based controls are intuitive and there is useful on-screen help for beginners, making this an easy way to get started with movie creation.

Audience

People of all ages who want to create their own movies and easily share them. Great for class projects and budding filmmakers.

Notes

1. http://we-envision.com/Page.asp?NavID=66.
2. http://mohawkcollege.ca.libguides.com/Apps.
3. http://liu.cwp.libguides.com/visualarts_apps.
4. Teaching the Catalog with Bamboo Paper: http://csslibrary.wordpress.com/2013/09/22/news-from-the-library-sept-23-2013/.
5. Five Simple Tips to Make Great Diptics: http://blog.dipticapp.com/2013/06/26/fives-simple-tips-to-make-great-diptics/.
6. An artist tells the story of how she uses Diptic: http://theappwhisperer.com/2013/01/28/portrayal-missing-home-by-jennifer-bracewell/.
7. http://www.adoberevel.com/apps/revel.
8. See the description of Pandora Radio in this book.
9. Read about the history of the Music Genome Project: http://en.wikipedia.org/wiki/Music_Genome_Project.
10. Pandora in car audio: https://www.pandora.com/everywhere/auto; and Pandora on your TV: https://tv.pandora.com/.
11. https://itunes.apple.com/us/book/garageband-for-ipad-how-it/id606651552?mt=11.
12. http://thumbjam.com/media.
13. Read about real ocarinas on Wikipedia: http://en.wikipedia.org/wiki/Ocarina.
14. http://www.smule.com/about.
15. http://www.smule.com/apps.
16. http://www.inmethod.com/airvideo/download.html.
17. http://www.inmethod.com/airvideo/remote-access.html.
18. http://en.wikipedia.org/wiki/Ken_Burns_effect.

CHAPTER 7

Apps for Social Media

Twitter and Other Social Media Updates

HootSuite for Twitter and Facebook

- Developer: HootSuite Media Inc., https://hootsuite.com/products/mobile-apps

- Version: 2.5.3

- Platforms: Android, iOS (universal)

- Price: Free

HootSuite is a social media app for Twitter, Facebook, Foursquare, and LinkedIn.

It's one of the best apps for Twitter, especially if you use multiple Twitter accounts. You can set up tabs for tweets, sent tweets, my tweets retweeted, mentions, direct messages, and more.

It's easy to search Twitter, see trending topics, and see stats on your Twitter accounts. You can set up tabs for multiple Twitter accounts and post under all of them. Easily save hashtag searches and view all the tweets, a handy feature when people are live tweeting events at conferences. You can choose from more than one retweet style, which is useful if you prefer the old way of retweeting.

You can also use it to view, comment, and "like" items on your Facebook news feed, view and comment on your Foursquare stream and check-in history, and view and post to your LinkedIn stream.

The pro version allows for unlimited social networks, more push notifications, and is ad-free. The free version is so good that if you don't mind ads, you may not need to upgrade.

Audience

This app is great for anyone who is managing social media updates for an organization (your library), or anyone who uses social media for their own professional life, or just for fun!

Examples

Jamyn Edis, professor at New York University's Stern School of Business, where he teaches new media marketing, uses HootSuite in a course he designed to give students social media marketing skills. Read more about his course in "How NYU's Stern School of Business Is Teaching Digital Skills with the Help of Codeacademy and HootSuite University."[1]

Other Apps Worth Trying

- Twitter: https://about.twitter.com/download. Android, iOS (universal).
- Pinterest: http://about.pinterest.com/goodies/. Android, iOS (universal).
- Google+: http://www.google.com/mobile/+/. Android, iOS (universal).
- Foursquare: https://foursquare.com/download/. Android, iOS. See full entry in this book.

Scheduling Your Social Media Updates

Buffer for Twitter and Facebook

- Developer: Buffer Inc., https://bufferapp.com/
- Version: 2.7.8
- Platforms: Android, iOS
- Price: Free

Buffer is a useful service for scheduling posts to all of your social media accounts. It provides link shortening and useful statistics. To use it, connect your various accounts (Twitter, Facebook, LinkedIn, App.net, and Google+ pages). Then set up your schedule for each account. You can select which hours and days of the week your posts will go out.

While browsing the web on your iPhone, use their mobile Safari bookmarklet to send a page directly to Buffer. You can also Buffer directly from other mobile apps, such as Feedly, Reeder, or Instapaper.[2] Buffer provides you with a private e-mail address to e-mail posts to your Buffer, so this makes it easy to post from other apps that don't have Buffer built in, such as Flipboard.[3]

Buffer works in your desktop or laptop web browser as well; visit http://bufferapp.com. Install the extensions for browsers you use to make it easy to post directly.[4]

Be sure to set up your schedule for each account in the app. If you've scheduled posts in the web version on your desktop or laptop, these won't carry over to the mobile app. If you want the times to match, set them up for each account in the app. You can set your time zone in the app, so that you're seeing the times in the zone you are in while traveling.

The free account allows you to post to one account for each service (one Twitter, one Facebook, etc.), and there is a paid account if you'd like more. It's called "The Awesome Plan" and is useful if you want two team members to post from the same account, posting to up to 12 profiles, varied schedules, and unlimited Buffer space.[5] There is also a Buffer for Business plan for even more features.[6]

The Buffer blog is worth following for advice on social media strategy, based on their extensive stats from everyone who uses Buffer. http://blog.bufferapp.com/.

Audience

Buffer is useful for anyone managing social media accounts who wants to post at optimal times and get detailed stats on their posts.

Managing Facebook Pages on the Go

Facebook Pages Manager

- Developer: Facebook Inc., https://www.facebook.com/appcenter/fbpagemanager_ios

- Version: 2.2

- Platforms: Android, iOS (universal)

- Price: Free

If you manage a Facebook page for your library, try the Facebook Pages Manager app. With this app you can get push notifications, reply to private messages, post updates, and post photos. This makes it easy to manage your page while away from your computer.

You can also view your Pages Insights and check-ins. See your total page likes, new page likes, post reach, people engaged, and more. If you have multiple pages to manage, you can do them all from this app.

For details, see the FAQ about the app.[7]

Audience

Use for anyone who manages Facebook Pages for their organization and wants to interact with it while away from their computer.

Example

Many libraries now have a Facebook page for their library. Seattle Public Library's Facebook page is a good example: https://www.facebook.com/SeattlePublicLibrary. This app is a good way to manage your page on the go.

Editing Your Blog

WordPress

- Developer: Automattic, http://ios.wordpress.org/
- Version: 3.8.6
- Platforms: Android, iOS (universal)
- Price: Free

The WordPress mobile app makes it easy to edit your blog while away from your computer. You can set it up to work with multiple blogs, either self-hosted or on Wordpress.com. Once you give it your Wordpress.com credentials, it will show all of your blogs on that site and you can select which ones to use in the app. For self-hosted blogs, enter the URL and log-in details for each one separately.

There is an easy interface for moderating comments, seeing your statistics, making edits to posts, and composing posts. There are buttons for adding HTML tags (lists, links, formatting, etc.), and it helps to know a little basic HTML because you'll see the tags in your text (it auto-inserts them). You can compose drafts, preview them, and also add images or videos.

This app is most useful for quick edits or creating drafts rather than composing everything from scratch. For that, WordPress on a desktop or laptop is easier.

There are other apps for blog editing (see the list below), so if you want to edit blogs on platforms other than WordPress, try those. If you want to try full-featured blog editing on your iPad, BlogPad Pro is a great choice, because the user interface is very intuitive compared to the others. It has a nice visual editor.

But for quick editing. moderating comments, and viewing stats, the free WordPress app is all you need.

Those who manage or contribute to blogs, both personal and organizational, and who want to draft posts, edit comments, and manage the blog on the go.

Examples

Many libraries use WordPress either as a blog or as a content management system for their website (or both). For support from an active community of libraries doing this, see the Facebook group WordPress and Librarians: https://www.facebook.com/groups/wordpress.librarians/.

Other Apps Worth Trying

All of the apps below are worth trying, and BlogPad Pro has the most intuitive user interface—useful for full-featured blog editing on the go.

- Tumblr: https://www.tumblr.com/. Android, iOS.

- BlogPress: http://blogpressapp.com/. iOS (universal).

- Blogsy for Wordpress, Blogger, and almost all blogging platforms: http://blogsyapp.com/. iOS (iPad only).

- BlogPad Pro: http://blogpadpro.com/. iOS (iPad only).

Sharing Photos with Filters

Instagram

- Developer: Instagram Inc., http://instagram.com/

- Version: 5.0.2

- Platforms: Android, iOS

- Price: Free

Instagram is a social photo-sharing app that makes it easy to share your photos, with interesting retro-looking filters applied. You can also share videos (up to 15 seconds long), with optional filters applied.

Sign up for an Instagram account and optionally connect to Facebook so you can see which of your friends are on Instagram and choose which ones to follow. You may also select from people in your phone's contact list or follow people from the "Instagram Suggested" list. You may follow anyone you like; they don't need to approve you, as on Facebook. Likewise, anyone can follow you.

Snap a photo or choose one you've already taken from your camera roll. Next, you'll be asked to scale and crop (choosing which area of your rectangular photo will show in the square—Instagram makes square photos). After that you can choose which filter you would like to apply (previewing each), or select none. Give your photo a caption and include hashtags if you like. Hashtags are keywords beginning with the # sign. They become clickable keywords, so that others can find your photo by searching with that word. Adding three to five relevant hashtags makes your photos more findable. You may also geotag the photo—tap "name this location" and the built-in geolocation will show you a list of nearby places that you can pick from. If you like, tag people in the photo and cross-post to other social networks (Facebook, Twitter, Tumblr, Foursquare, or Flickr). You can turn on a button "add to photo map" and your photos will show on a map. This is a nice way to browse all your photos taken in different locations while traveling.

Once you finish and tap "share," your photo goes into your stream for your followers to see. People can "like" or comment on your photos, and you can reply in the comments.

Instagram is a fun way to find interesting images and share your photos with the world or just a few friends. If you tap the "explore" button, you can browse, or search by user or hashtag. You can elect to get push notifications whenever someone likes or comments on your photos.

Many people use Instagram as a way to visually comment on interesting things around them, adding humorous hashtags and responding to comments. It's fun to search by color, by season, by place, or by popular events that are happening right now, such as #olympics2014.

For some especially interesting photos, follow NASA: http://instagram.com/nasa; the U.S. Department of the Interior: http://instagram.com/usinterior/; or a photographer called 02q from Tokyo, Japan: http://instagram.com/02q.

Audience

Anyone who wants to enjoy photography with filters and participate in social commentary about photos with friends and followers.

Examples

Libraries are doing fun things with Instagram to promote their library and to interact with their user community. For example, the Lloyd Sealy Library at the John Jay College of Criminal Justice at CUNY uses Instagram to post old-time mug shots in their collections ("Mugshot Mondays"), and photos from their special collections related to the history of John Jay and criminal justice ("Throwback Thursdays").[8] They report that cross-posting these to Facebook gets the best traction.

Sharing and Organizing Your Photos

Flickr

- Developer: Yahoo, https://mobile.yahoo.com/flickr
- Version: 2.32.1556
- Platforms: Android, iOS
- Price: Free

Flickr is a social network for serious photographers, owned by Yahoo. It's a full-featured place to store and share your photos, either publicly or privately.

Flickr's mobile app makes it easy to shoot and upload directly from your mobile phone. Everyone gets a free terabyte of data, so there is plenty of storage space. If you like, you can set it to auto-upload all of your photos in the background (with the option to do it only when you're on Wi-Fi, to save on cellular data). The photos will stay private until you have a chance to select which ones you want to make public.

When you shoot a photo in the Flickr app, you can edit it or add filters (similar to Instagram) before uploading. In the photo editor you can adjust brightness, saturation, sharpness, and contrast. You can also crop it, rotate it, and use other typical photo-editing tools.

When you have a Flickr account, you can add your friends or anyone as contacts, following their photos. You can also join groups on various topics of interest, such as "window seat please," "altered signs," "libraries and librarians," "waterfalls," and many more. Groups have various rules about how many and what kinds of photos you can contribute to the group. They are a great way to share your photos and find others on areas of common interest.

Mark photos belonging to anyone as "favorites," create sets of your own photos, and create collections (groupings of your sets). In the mobile app you can browse your sets, groups, favorites, and the people you are following. Tap the globe icon and you'll see Flickr's "interesting" collection, a curated set of some of the most beautiful and interesting photos on Flickr. Tap the "nearby" button and see photos taken near where you are right now.

Audience

Serious photographers or anyone who enjoys photography and wants to share and find photos.

Examples

Many libraries have accounts on Flickr and use it to publicize their collections, buildings, and activities. The Boston Public Library has many interesting sets on Flickr,[9] including documents from special collections, like these antislavery broadsides (http://www.flickr.com/photos/boston_public_library/sets/72157632595313718/) and beautiful vintage travel posters (http://www.flickr.com/photos/boston_public_library/sets/72157624587860480/).

For more ideas on using Flickr, see this article by P. F. Anderson, "31 Flavors: Things to Do with Flickr in Libraries."[10]

Other Apps Worth Trying

- 500px: http://500px.com/apps. Android, iOS (universal).

Notes

1. "How NYU's Stern School of Business Is Teaching Digital Skills with the Help of Codecademy & HootSuite University," http://blog.hootsuite.com/nyustern-digital-skills/.

2. See complete list of apps that connect with Buffer here: http://bufferapp.com/extras.

3. Instructions for finding your private Buffer e-mail address: http://bufferapp.com/guides/email.

4. Browser extensions for Buffer: http://bufferapp.com/extensions.

5. Details on Buffer's Awesome Plan: https://bufferapp.com/faq#awesome-plan-vs-free-plan.

6. Details on Buffer for Business: https://bufferapp.com/business.

7. Facebook Pages Manager FAQ: https://m.facebook.com/pages_manager/help?_rdr.

8. Emerging Tech in Libraries blog: http://emerging.commons.gc.cuny.edu/2013/09/using-instagram-library/.

9. Boston Public Library sets on Flickr: http://www.flickr.com/photos/boston_public_library/sets/.

10. "31 Flavors: Things to Do with Flickr in Libraries," http://www.webjunction.org/documents/webjunction/31_Flavors_045_Things_to_Do_With_Flickr_in_Libraries.html.

CHAPTER 8

Apps for Communication

Audio and Video Calls over the Internet

Skype

- Developer: Skype Communications, http://www.skype.com/
- Version: 4.15.1
- Platforms: Android, iOS
- Price: Free

Skype features free video and voice calls and instant messaging to other Skype users on desktop computers or mobile devices. You can also send files, photos, and videos and share your screen.

For a small fee you can call mobile phones and landlines worldwide, or make group video calls with up to 10 people. With a premium account you can do group screen sharing with up to 10 people.

Audience

Anyone who wants to communicate with others worldwide for free (Skype to Skype) or at a very low cost (Skype to mobile and landlines).

Examples

Some libraries use Skype to offer reference service. Madison Area Technical College in Madison, Wisconsin, has a useful guide for how this works at their library; see: http://libguides.madisoncollege.edu/Skype.

They offer video or voice calls, instant messaging, and sometimes use screen sharing to answer questions.

Other libraries offer virtual author visits using Skype. The Prescott Public Library in Arizona saved money by inviting teen author K. L. Going to chat with teens using Skype. Paying for her to visit in person would have been cost-prohibitive. Teens in Arizona enjoyed asking questions of her while she was sitting at home in New York. This successful program led to the development of a "Teen Author Skype Series" at the Prescott Public Library.[1]

Other Apps Worth Trying

- VSee: http://vsee.com/ (HIPAA- compliant). Android, iOS.

One-on-One or Group Video Chats

Hangouts

- Developer: Google Inc., http://support.google.com/hangouts?p=ioshelp
- Version: 1.3.2
- Platforms: Android, iOS (universal)
- Price: Free

Google's app for one-on-one or group conversations includes several features that make it useful for collaborating:

- Use with any combination of phones, tablets, and computers.
- Make video calls for up to 10 people.
- Sync conversations across all your devices.
- Save your video call history.
- Enable screen sharing for collaboration.
- Integrate your Google Drive documents, so you can see them while chatting.

Stream your Hangouts live and in public to YouTube, and save a copy for those who want to watch later.

Audience

Hangouts is useful for anyone who wants to collaborate or chat at a distance.

Examples

Libraries are using Hangouts in several interesting ways. The New York Public Library uses it for a virtual book club; see "NYPL's 'Gone Girl' Hangout": http://www.youtube.com/watch?v=DNRjTs7cbTA. Some library professional groups use it to host virtual lightning talks; see "How to Host Your Own Virtual Lightning Talks Using Google Hangout," by Peter Murray: http://www.slideshare.net/DataGazetteer/lightning-talks-with-google-hangout. Some librarians use it to conduct office hours and library instruction remotely; see "Using Google Hangouts (with extras) for Office Hours 2011" by Alison Hicks, romance language librarian at University of Colorado: http://www.colorado.edu/oit/academic-technology/blog/using-google-hangouts-extras-office-hours-fall 2011.

For a useful summary of how this works, see "Using Google Hangouts for Newbies" by P. F. Anderson: http://etechlib.wordpress.com/2013/01/30/using-google-hangouts-for-newbies/.

Other Apps Worth Trying

- Google Voice: http://www.google.com/support/voice/. Android, iOS.

Instant Messaging

imo free video calls and chat

- Developer: imo.im, https://imo.im/
- Version: 3.11.2
- Platforms: Android, iOS (universal)
- Price: Free

Imo is an app for free chat and audio or video calls over Wi-Fi and cellular. It aggregates other instant messaging networks, including Facebook chat, Google Talk, AIM, Yahoo! Messenger, ICQ, Jabber, and more. As long as the person you want to chat with also has imo, you can communicate for free. Create groups, share photos, or just chat with your friends on different networks.

Imo is a way to sign in to just one service for communicating with everyone you know on different services. Set up a free account, and then sign in to your accounts on other services within the app and it will remember you. The app will send you a push notification when one of your friends wants to chat.

Audience

People who want a free way to chat with friends on various networks.

Free Cross-Platform Text Messaging

WhatsApp Messenger

- Developer: WhatsApp Inc., http://www.whatsapp.com/
- Version: 2.11.7
- Platforms: Android, iOS
- Price: Free for the first year; $0.99/year after that

WhatsApp is a cross-platform messaging app for exchanging messages without having to pay for SMS. As long as everyone in the conversation has the app, you can send an unlimited number of text messages, audio and video messages, photos and videos, and group chats.

It works on iPhone, Android, Blackberry, Windows phone, and Nokia. You can create groups of friends and send a broadcast message to them (one-to-many). Or you can set up a group conversation with up to 30 people at once (many-to-many). It works on both Wi-Fi and cellular connections and there are no international charges. It connects automatically with the address book on your phone and displays all of your contacts who also have WhatsApp. It uses your own phone number instead of setting up a special number like some other messaging apps.

You can have it send push notifications when you have a message, and if you turn off notifications, it will save the messages for you until the next time you open the app. "Share location" sends a small map of where you are now to the person you're chatting with. Clicking on the small map opens it in your phone's mapping app.

If you want to save a particular chat's history, that's easy to do with the "email conversation" link. On iPhones, you can choose to have it automatically back up your chats to iCloud or to back up selectively on demand.

You may have heard about Facebook's purchase of WhatsApp. According to the WhatsApp blog, they will operate as an independent unit within Facebook and nothing will change about the app.[2]

Audience

WhatsApp is great for those on a budget who want to communicate without getting charged for messaging. It's especially great for those who need to communicate internationally.

Example

The Hong Kong University of Science and Technology Library[3] is using WhatsApp to provide reference service, supplementing their existing forms of communication. Since smartphones are very common among students and staff, they are adding this service. Librarians connect to it using an Android emulator on one of their staff computers. They offer it during the same hours as their e-mail service. For more information, see their newsletter article "WhatsApp a Librarian!": http://library.ust.hk/info/notes/notes91.html#whatsapp.

Other Apps Worth Trying

- GroupMe: https://groupme.com/. Android, iOS (universal).

Notes

1. "Plan an Author Visit Using Skype," http://childrensbooks.about.com/od/visits/a/Plan-An-Author-Visit-Using-Skype.htm.
2. http://blog.whatsapp.com/499/Facebook.
3. http://library.ust.hk/.

CHAPTER 9

Apps for Content Creation and Curation

Creating Presentations

Keynote

- Developer: Apple, http://www.apple.com/ios/keynote/
- Version: 2.0.1
- Platforms: iOS (universal)
- Price: $9.99 (free with new iOS device purchase)

Keynote is an easy-to-use presentation app similar to PowerPoint. It comes with a set of well-designed themes, and pro themes are available from several publishers as well. This makes it easy to design great-looking presentations.

You can create presentations via the app, but you might prefer to create on the desktop where more features are available and then copy it to your iPad via either iTunes or iCloud.

When presenting, use a VGA dongle to plug your iPad into the projector, or if you have Apple TV, you can wirelessly stream to your Apple TV plugged into a projector, so you can walk around the room. (See the section in this book, Apple TV with AirPlay).

It's friendly with PowerPoint because you can export your slides as PowerPoint or as PDF. You can also open PowerPoint slides that others have sent you. For more details, see Apple's information about Keynote and PowerPoint compatibility.[1]

Audience

Keynote is useful for anyone who wants to easily create professional-looking presentations.

Presenting PowerPoint Slides

SlideShark Presentation App

- Developer: Brainshark Inc., https://www.slideshark.com/
- Version: 3.3.0
- Platforms: iOS (universal)
- Price: Free; Pro accounts available: $49/year for 500 MB, $95/year for 1 GB

SlideShark is an app for presenting PowerPoint slides using the iPad. Create your slides on the desktop and import them from cloud services, such as Dropbox, SkyDrive, or Box, or open email-attached PowerPoint files with the "open in . . ." command. You can also get a free cloud account on SlideShark for up to 100 MB, so you can upload your slide decks from your computer. Get more storage for referring friends.

SlideShark preserves fonts and graphics without mangling them, which can happen in other apps. See your slide's notes, timers, and next/previous slides. You can show embedded videos, draw on your slides, and highlight content, all while presenting. Turn your iPhone into a remote control with the built-in virtual laser pointer.

It doesn't work as a Keynote presenter (Keynote itself is better for that), but you can export Keynote slides as PowerPoint and work from there.

SlideShark also allows you to broadcast your slides in real time to a remote audience using the Pro or Team version. For details, including pricing, see SlideShark's website[2]—free version for up to three people, or pay for more. A team edition is also available.

Audience

SlideShark is useful for those who want to present PowerPoint presentations using an iPad.

Creating Simple, Beautiful Presentations

Haiku Deck

- Developer: Haiku Deck Inc., http://www.haikudeck.com/
- Version: 2.4
- Platforms: iOS (universal)
- Price: Free

Haiku Deck allows you to create presentations with an elegant, minimalist look. One unique and useful feature is its ability to search Creative Commons–licensed images[3] to use in your slides. Built-in themes are included, with premium themes available.

Haiku Deck includes a wide selection of fonts, image filters, and layouts— all you need to make your slides look beautiful. It's easy to make charts and graphs. Share your decks via Facebook, Twitter, or e-mail; post to your blog; or export as PowerPoint, Keynote, or PDF.

It also has a free web version,[4] so you can create presentations in your web browser on your desktop or laptop. You can publish your slides on HaikuDeck.com with one of three options: public, restricted (only those who have the link can view it), or private (only you can view your deck).

View HaikuDeck.com's gallery for featured and popular decks.

Audience

Anyone who wants to create elegant presentations with a minimalist look.

Examples

For an example of an excellent presentation made with Haiku Deck, see "Graduate Student Library Orientation," by Bob Fraser of Mardigian Library at University of Michigan, Dearborn: http://www.haikudeck.com/p/L0fRlKSf10/graduate-student-library-orientation.

Other Apps Worth Trying

- Prezi: http://prezi.com/ipad/. iOS (iPad). App for creating presentations on a zooming, virtual canvas. People either love or hate Prezi. See this list for some examples: http://blog.crazyegg.com/2012/10/29/example-presentations-using-prezi/.

Creating Interactive Books Very Easily

Book Creator for iPad

- Developer: Red Jumper Studio, http://www.redjumper.net/bookcreator/

- Version: 3.0.1

- Platforms: Android, iOS (universal)

- Price: $4.99; 50 percent discount for educational institutions purchasing 20 or more copies[5]

Book Creator is an easy-to-use app for creating multimedia eBooks. With it you can create eBooks that include text, images, video, music, and narration.

It's very easy to get started. Just tap the "+" button to create a new book (portrait, square, or landscape layouts available). Then tap the "+" at the top of the screen to add content, such as photos, text, sounds, or a pen tool for writing and drawing on your pages. At any time you can preview your book by opening it in iBooks on your iPad.

Books are made in "fixed-layout" format, so it's best for books where the images are primary, like cookbooks, children's picture books, photo books, or art books. It's an easy tool for kids to use, so many teachers are using it for classroom projects.

When you're ready to publish your book, you can share your finished book for free with friends and colleagues (it's an EPUB file), by sharing through Dropbox, Google Drive, or the like. You can also make your book available in Apple's iBooks store under either a free or a paid account.[6]

Audience

Book Creator is great for kids or anyone who wants to create a multimedia eBook without needing to learn more complex authoring tools.

Examples

Jon Smith, technology integration specialist for Alliance City Schools, used Book Creator with a class of autistic boys in fourth grade. This successful project resulted in several books created by these students. Read about the details in "Using Book Creator to Support Autistic Students," http://www.redjumper.net/blog/2014/01/using-book-creator-support-autistic-students/.

Professional artist Andy Maitland used Book Creator as an easy way to publish a book of his art. Read his story in "iPad Artist Goes from Blank Canvas to Published eBook," http://www.redjumper.net/blog/2013/12/ipad-artist-goes-blank-canvas-published-ebook/.

Librarian Karin Hallett of the Martin J. Gottlieb Day School in Jacksonville, Florida, uses Book Creator to create history eBooks with her students. Read more in "Creating and Publishing a Collaborative eBook," http://www.redjumper.net/blog/2013/10/creating-publishing -collaborative-ebook/.

See also a Pinterest board that showcases books made with Book Creator: http://www.pinterest.com/bookcreator/made-in-book-creator/.

Creating Interactive Books for Apple's iBookstore

iBooks Author

- Developer: Apple, http://www.apple.com/ibooks-author/
- Version: 2.1.1
- Platforms: Mac OS
- Price: Free

Even though this is not a mobile app (it runs on Macs), iBooks Author is important to know about, because with it you can creative interactive eBooks for Apple's iBookstore with multimedia features for viewing on iPads.

iBooks Author's strengths are that it's easy to learn, easy to use, and free. It includes templates that make it easy to create a beautiful, interactive book. The weakness is that these books run on only Apple's platform.

However, that's not a deal breaker because you can export a version of your book without the interactive content and make it available on other platforms, such as Kindle, Nook, or a PDF available from your own website.

iBooks Author was created with textbook design in mind. It's perfect for setting up a curriculum of ordered course materials, with interactive charts and graphs, slideshows, embedded videos, and quizzes. It's also useful for other types of books that benefit from interactive content, such as travel guides, cookbooks, museum catalogs, and more.

You can make your book available for free in Apple's iBookstore, or you can sell it, getting 70 percent of sales while Apple gets 30 percent (the same amount that app developers get). Having your books in Apple's store makes them available to a large audience of iPad users.

To browse through the catalog of books, open iTunes, click on "Books," then look for a link (usually in Quick Links) called "made for iBooks."

That brings you to the section of books made with iBooks Author—books with interactive content.

For more information on working with iBooks Author, see my presentation that was given at MIT in January 2012—"iBooks Author: Creating Multi-Touch Books for iPad."[7]

Audience
Professors, students, and any author who wants to create interactive books for iPad.

Examples
Some libraries are using iBooks Author to create free interactive books from their digital collections. The New York Public Library is an excellent example of this with their digital publication called *Point*.[8] It's a series of publications on different topics, each with historical photos, maps, and prints surrounded by text that provides context for the materials.

Here are two examples from this series:

- *NYPL Point: Frankenstein, Making a Modern Monster*[9]: New York Public Library, free
- *NYPL Point: John Cage's Prepared Piano*[10]: New York Public Library, free

Screencasting and Interactive Whiteboards

Explain Everything
- Developer: MorrisCooke, http://www.explaineverything.com/
- Version: 2.31
- Platforms: Android, iOS (iPad only)
- Price: $2.99; also available in Apple's Volume Purchase program with 50 percent discount for educators[11]

Explain Everything is for creating screencasts (or live demos) of annotated documents, drawing, photos, or videos on your iPad.

Open it, select a template (color scheme), and then type or draw on your iPad. Choose from a pencil tool, shape tool (circles, rectangles, lines, stars), or insert photos, movies, or documents to annotate. Hold down on a tool to change it—for example, the shape tool has options for shadows and border, the type tool options for font, size, and border.

What makes this app more interesting than simple annotation apps is that you can record your actions to make a screencast. At any time, tap the "record" button and it will record what you're doing on the screen. Annotate photos or documents, illustrate a series of steps or instructions, or insert slides made in PowerPoint and narrate them. You can record your voice or insert music that you have previously saved on your device. You can even insert movies and draw or type over them while they are playing, making comments about what's going on in the movie. Also, a built-in web browser lets you import web pages and annotate them.

At any time, you can save your project within the app for future editing. You can also export individual pages as images to your camera roll, e-mail, or as a PDF to iBooks. You can export your screencasts to the camera roll or YouTube.

If you connect the app to your cloud services, you can save a whole project or individual pages (as video, PDF, image file, or project) to Dropbox, Evernote, Google Drive, Box, SkyDrive, Vimeo, or a WebDav server. You can also import files from these services as a way to begin your project.

If you want to do a live demo, you can attach your iPad to a projector or stream it to Apple TV connected to a large screen or projector. Then talk and annotate your slides in front of a live audience or classroom. The developer provides a series of video tutorials on their website to demonstrate the various features of this app; see: http://www.morriscooke.com/?p=1045.

Audience

Teachers or professors who want to create demonstrations or screencasts. Students at all levels who need to create showcases of what they've learned. Anyone who wants to create a screencast that illustrate a technique or concept.

Examples

An MIT professor used Explain Everything to create drawings and animations for a video preview of her edX course. See her video here: http://youtu.be/BHI-xk84Cv4.

Math teacher Jennifer Kimbrell used Explain Everything with student assignments where they were asked to make short videos showing how they solved their math problems. Read the full story on her blog, *Teach with Jen*: http://blog.techwithjen.com/2013/10/using-explain-everything -for-daily-math.html.

Other Apps Worth Trying

- Doceri Interactive Whiteboard: http://doceri.com/. iOS (iPad only). Another popular and useful interactive whiteboard app.

Creating Designs for 3D Printing

123D Design

- Developer: Autodesk Inc., http://www.123dapp.com/design

- Version: 1.4

- Platforms: iOS (iPad only)

- Price: Free

3D printing is the process of making a physical object from a digital model. It's used to create a variety of items, such as prototypes of inventions, household objects, replacement parts, or art. It's on the rise, with the cost of 3D printers coming down in recent years.

Some libraries are experimenting with offering 3D printing as a service to their patrons, usually as part of a "makerspace."[12] In addition to desktop software for creating 3D models, there are mobile apps for designing in 3D.

Autodesk makes several apps in this area. 123D Design is a good place to start. With it you can start your design on your iPad, save it in the cloud, and finish it on your desktop with 123D Design for Mac or Windows.[13]

You can select from premade shapes and then modify them by adding additional parts, pieces, and shapes, all of which are modifiable with various taps and swipes on your iPad. Some aspects of designing on an iPad feel more intuitive than using the same software on a desktop or laptop, because you can touch the screen instead of using a mouse.

Several video tutorials are available on Autodesk's site,[14] and they are worth watching to get an idea of how this type of software works, even if you don't plan to create your own designs.

If you want to experiment with 3D printing but don't have access to a printer,[15] you can send your designs to an online service that will print and ship to you. Examples include Shapeways,[16] Sculpeo,[17] and iMaterialise.[18]

To learn more, see these tutorials at http://www.123dapp.com/howto/design, and instructional videos at https://www.youtube.com/user/123d/videos.

Autodesk makes several other apps related to 3D printing.

- 123D Creature: http://www.123dapp.com/creature. Create and print fantastic characters. iOS (iPad only).

- 123D Sculpt: http://www.123dapp.com/sculpt. Tactile modeling for iPad. iOS (iPad only).

- 123D Catch: http://www.123dapp.com/catch. Generate 3D models from photos. iOS (universal).

- 123D Make Intro: http://www.123dapp.com/make. Unique 3D models from 2D slices. iOS (universal).

If you're in doubt about the role libraries have to play in 3D printing, or if you want to advocate for it in your library, see "3D Printing: Is it for Libraries?" in Phil Bradley's blog: http://philbradley.typepad.com/phil _bradleys_weblog/2013/01/3d-printing-is-it-for-libraries.html.

Audience

People of all ages who would like to get started with creating and modifying 3D designs.

Examples

On Instructables, Autodesk has a group of project instructions for items you can create with your 3D printer: http://www.instructables.com/group/123D/.

Other Apps Worth Trying

- Makies FabLab: http://makie.me/, iOS (iPad only). Build fully customizable digital dolls. See "Libby, the librarian" at http://makie.me/ forum/topic/348-libby-the-librarian/?page=1#post-5844. Librarian action figures, anyone?

- Blokify—3D Printing & Modeling: http://blokify.com/. iOS (universal). Easily create 3D models made with customizable "bloks."

- Thingiverse: http://www.thingiverse.com/. Android, iOS. A community for discovery and sharing 3D creations.

Curating Web Content

Flipboard

- Developer: Flipboard Inc., https://flipboard.com/

- Version: 2.2.2

- Platforms: Android, iOS (universal)

- Price: Free

Flipboard is a visual news-reading app that provides an appealing way to browse, read, and share stories from a variety of sources. Swipe pages to the right on your iPad (or up on your iPhone) and they flip like the pages of a book, rather than scrolling like web pages. Tap on a title to read a full story, at which point you can scroll down. Stories can be "liked," or shared by e-mail, messaging, Facebook, Twitter, or Google+. You can also save stories to Instapaper, save images to your camera roll, or open the page in Safari.

The flipping interface makes the images for each story very prominent, so it's an appealing way to browse through stories where the images are important. Topics like interior design, photography, travel, art, and cooking work especially well in this type of interface.

To set up your Flipboard, you can choose from general topics, such as News, Business, Tech & Science, Music, or Books. Within each general topic are specific sources and subtopics. Select the ones you like and your Flipboard will fill with a box for each one. In addition, you can search for and add particular Twitter feeds or lists, hashtags (such as #longreads), and stories or posts from social media, such as Google+, YouTube, Flickr, or Instagram. You can browse your own Facebook and other social media feeds as well, if you connect them to Flipboard. For example, you can browse your "favorites" on Flickr—it's an appealing way to browse and share photos you've previously favorited.

One of the most interesting features is the ability to create your own "magazines" on any topics you like. To create one, click the "+" sign on any story and you will be able to make a new magazine. Give your magazine a name and description and then you can "flip" stories into it by tapping the "+" on stories in Flipboard.

There are other ways to add stories—browse the web on your mobile device and copy the link to a web page, then open the Flipboard app. It will ask you if you want to add that story to one of your magazines. In your desktop web browser, you can install a bookmarklet ("+Flip it") that will copy any web page into one of your magazines.[19] Tap it when you're on the page you want to include and you'll be asked to select one of the images and which of your magazines to add the story to.

Once you're created a magazine, you can choose which story becomes the cover (pick one with an attractive image), and you can share it on social media so others can subscribe to it for free. You can also browse magazines that others have created and subscribe to the ones of interest.

Flipboard is an appealing way to curate and aggregate content in a way that is easy to browse and makes the images prominent. I have found it useful to select very specific subtopics of interest, rather than choosing more general topics that I'm reading in other news sources. I turn to Flipboard when I want to browse those specific topics.

Audience

People who want to browse the news in a visually appealing way. Anyone who wants to create a "magazine" on a specific topic to share with others.

Examples

Librarians can make Flipboard "magazines" on any number of topics, including booklists or advocacy for their library. Here is one by Jan Holmquist[20] called "What's New in the World of Libraries" at https://flipboard.com/section/libraries-bz2m37.

I have created a Flipboard magazine about interactive eBooks for the iPad called "Book as App—Interactive, Multi-Touch" at http://flip.it/pkjSw.

Librarian Linda Braun made a useful screencast tutorial, "Create Your Own Magazines with Flipboard."[21]

Scoop.it

- Developer: Scoop.it Inc., http://www.scoop.it/
- Version: 2.1.0
- Platforms: Android, iOS (a separate version of the app is available for iPad)
- Price: Free

Scoop.it is a content curation tool available on the web at http://www.scoop.it/. Use it to collect stories on a topic that you can share via a "magazine" on the web. If you connect your social media accounts, you can simultaneously send your "scoops" out to them as well. Sign up for a free account and you can create up to two curated topics ("magazines") and connect to up to two social media sources (such as Facebook and Twitter). Paid accounts enable you to create and use more topics and sources. You can also choose to follow magazines that others have created on topics you're interested in.

In order to set up a new topic, use the desktop website. Search for and add sources from particular RSS feeds, Twitter accounts and lists, Scoop.it topics, YouTube videos, SlideShare decks, and more. Then browse the stories from your selected sources and "scoop" the ones you want into your magazine. You may add your own summary or comments, if you like. To keep your magazine up to date, view these stories on a regular schedule, and add relevant ones to your magazine.

After your topics are created, you can manage them using the mobile app. Pick one of your topics, tap "curate," and you'll see the stories from your sources. View each story and "scoop" the ones you want to add to your magazine. You can also view your magazine in the mobile app and view the magazines that you follow. The mobile apps make it easy to maintain your magazine while away from your computer.

Audience

Anyone who wants to curate stories on specific topics and post to multiple social media accounts.

Examples

Librarians are making "Scoop.its" on interesting topics. For example, "Innovative Libraries" at http://www.scoop.it/t/innovative-libraries, and "Social Media and Libraries" at http://www.scoop.it/t/social-media-and -libraries by Trudy Raymakers.

Wirelessly Show the Display of iOS Devices on a Large Screen

Apple TV with AirPlay

- Developer: Apple, http://www.apple.com/appletv/, http://www.apple.com/appletv/airplay/
- Platforms: iOS (iPad only)
- Price: $99.00

One of the easiest ways to show the screen of your iOS devices on a large screen is with an Apple TV connected to a projector or large-screen television with HDMI input. Using Apple's AirPlay technology, you can easily mirror the display of an instructor's iPad and then switch to the display of any iPad or iPhone belonging to students in your workshop. Because it's all wireless, the instructor can easily move around the room.

Apple TV is a small black box that fits in the palm of your hand. You will also need to purchase an HDMI cable to connect Apple TV to your projector or large-screen TV.[22] Just tap the AirPlay icon in any AirPlay-enabled app (such as Photos, Videos, or Safari) and it will show on the big screen. All of your devices need to be on the same Wi-Fi network for this to work.[23] You can also mirror the entire display, including home screen and any app, by using the AirPlay mirroring feature as described here: http://support.apple.com/kb/ht5209.

If you don't have an HDMI projector, you can still connect your iPad directly to it using a VGA connector, but then you won't have the advantage of being able to move around the room or show the display of any student easily. Since many venues have only VGA projectors, some have written about how to find an adaptor that works between your Apple TV and the projector, which will allow you to work wirelessly.[24]

Apple TV also includes YouTube, Flickr, Vimeo, and iTunes U, making it easy to project from those sources. You can also take photos and show them via Photo Stream (Apple's service for instantly syncing photos on all your devices), with almost live updating as the photos are taken. This is great for group projects involving photos.

At the time of this writing, unfortunately there is not an easy way to mirror Android devices wirelessly. There are a few apps that enable this if you "root" your device, such as MirrorOp Sender.[25] Google has announce that Chromecast will add this feature later in 2014, so it may be available by the time you read this.

Audience

Anyone doing group presentations or workshops with Apple iOS devices who wants a wireless solution.

Example

The University of Minnesota has a useful page of instructions for how to set up Apple TV to project your iPad.[26]

Other Apps Worth Trying

- If you want to mirror iOS devices wirelessly to a computer hooked up to a projector (instead of using Apple TV), try Reflector, a Mac or Windows app described in the next entry.

Mirror Your iOS Devices on Your Mac or Windows PC

Reflector

- Developer: Squirrels, http://www.airsquirrels.com/reflector/
- Platforms: Mac OS X or Windows
- Price: $12.99 for a single user, $54.99 for multiseat (five licenses)

Reflector is a handy app for your Mac or Windows PC that allows you to mirror the display of your iOS device on your computer. (Your devices need to be on the same Wi-Fi network.) It uses Apple's built-in AirPlay technology to enable this.[27]

With it you can easily demonstrate apps or make screencasts showing how particular apps work. Everything happening on your iOS device is mirrored, including the audio. When you change orientation of your device, that is also reflected on your computer's screen.

Another interesting feature is the ability to mirror multiple devices on the same computer screen at once. This is an interesting way to compare the screen of two different apps or to have a friendly competition between different people on a screen for everyone to see.

Reflector also has a built-in recording feature for recording what's happening on your desktop's screen, making it easy to create instructional screencasts about iOS apps.[28] You could also record your screen with a more full-featured screencasting app, such as ScreenFlow for Mac[29] or Camtasia for Windows.[30]

For more details, see "AirPlay in the Classroom: Apple TV vs Reflector App."[31]

Be aware also, that Apple has announced another way to mirror devices when iOS 8 and Mac OS X Yosemite are available, likely by the time you read this. If you have this setup, you may be able to easily mirror your devices on a Mac using a lightning cable (without need for the Reflector app), as described in this article: "OS X Yosemite Lets You Video Capture iOS8 Devices with a Lightning Cable" at http://www.idownloadblog.com /2014/06/03/yosemite-ios-8-screenscasting/.

Notes

1. http://www.apple.com/ios/keynote/compatibility/.
2. https://www.slideshark.com/products/broadcast-feature-remote -presentations.
3. More information about Creative Commons licensing: http://creative commons.org/about.
4. http://www.haikudeck.com/account/signin?newdeck=1.
5. If a developer has enabled education pricing, your institution can get 50 percent off when purchasing 20 or more copies through Apple's Volume Purchase Program: http://www.apple.com/education/it/vpp/.
6. Apple's FAQ for book authors and publishers: http://www.apple.com/itunes/ working-itunes/sell-content/books/book-faq.html.
7. http://www.slideshare.net/nic221/ibooks-author-creating-multitouch -books-for-ipad.
8. http://www.nypl.org/point.
9. https://itunes.apple.com/us/book/nypl-point-frankenstein-making/ id572663054?mt=11.

10. https://itunes.apple.com/us/book/nypl-point-john-cages-prepared/id559342852?mt=11.

11. http://www.apple.com/itunes/education/. Search for "morriscooke" in the volume purchase program app store.

12. Some examples of libraries offering 3D printing: Westport Public Library: http://westportlibrary.org/services/maker-space/3d-printers; Northbrook Public Library: http://www.northbrook.info/3d-printing; Cleveland Public Library: http://www.cpl.org/EventsClasses/3DPrinting.aspx; and NCSU Libraries: http://www.lib.ncsu.edu/spaces/makerspace.

13. Watch this video for a demo of 123D Design on the iPad: https://www.youtube.com/watch?v=3M3q7vTd-Ko.

14. More video tutorials on 123D Design: http://www.123dapp.com/howto/design.

15. Online 3D printing services: http://www.123dapp.com/3d-printing-services.

16. Shapeways: http://www.shapeways.com/123d_welcome.

17. Sculpeo: http://www.sculpteo.com/.

18. iMaterialise: http://i.materialise.com/.

19. Instructions for the Flip It bookmarklet: https://share.flipboard.com/p/mobilebookmarklet.

20. http://janholmquist.net/about/.

21. http://www.thedigitalshift.com/2013/04/software/create-your-own-magazines-with-flipboard-screencast-tutorial/.

22. Good HDMI cables are not expensive: http://thewirecutter.com/reviews/best-hdmi-cables/. Details from Apple about cables needed: http://support.apple.com/kb/HT4366.

23. If you are in a location that uses different subnets, you may not actually have all your devices on the same network. An inexpensive work-around is to purchase a small travel router like this one at http://www.amazon.com/gp/product/B007PTCFFW and connect your devices to your own network.

24. Description of how to use a special adapter to connect your Apple TV to a VGA projector: http://ipadacademy.com/2012/06/connect-your-ipad-to-a-projector-go-wireless-with-apple-tv-airplay-mirroring.

25. MirrorOp Sender for Android: https://play.google.com/store/apps/details?id=com.awindinc.sphone2tv&hl=en.

26. http://www.classroom.umn.edu/support/appletv.html.

27. See a list of devices that support AirPlay here: http://www.airsquirrels.com/reflector/compatible-devices/.

28. How recording works in Reflector: http://blog.airsquirrels.com/post/66120831461/record-your-ipad-or-iphone-with-reflector.

29. Screenflow for Mac: http://www.telestream.net/screenflow/overview.htm.

30. Camtasia for Windows: http://www.techsmith.com/camtasia.html.

31. http://professorjosh.com/2013/02/17/airplay-in-the-classroom-apple-tv-vs-reflector-app/.

CHAPTER 10

Apps for Showcasing Special Collections

Showcasing Special Collections

NYPL Biblion: World's Fair

- Developer: New York Public Library, http://www.nypl.org/node/118129

- Version: 1.6.1

- Platforms: iOS (iPad only)

- Price: Free

The New York Public Library has created a collections-based app called Biblion: The Boundless Library. It's designed to feature items from special collections, giving them context by adding essays and historical information to a collection of photographs, movies, documents, and recordings that can be easily navigated on your iPad. The first edition, "World's Fair," is a collection of the official corporate records of the 1939–40 New York World's Fair.[1]

"Stacks view" allows you to easily browse through multimedia content by swiping through photos and videos. It appears when you hold the iPad in landscape orientation. Turn to portrait orientation and see the "book view," with stories that give background and interesting facts about each part of the collection. Stories are by various authors, such as Henry

Jenkins and Elliott Kalan, with links to more information about them and their writings on the NYPL website.

Tapping on an icon in the top bar brings you to a 3D view of all the themes in the collection, making it easy to skip to the parts you are most interested in. Themes include: Enter the World of Tomorrow; Fashion, Food and Famous Faces; From the Stacks; You Ain't Seen Nothin' Yet; A Moment in Time; and Beacon of Idealism. A particularly fun and interesting section is the gallery, "Mad Science—Robots, Mechanical Dogs, and Incubators." Browse photos of "Elektro, the Westinghouse Moto-Man," and his robot dog, "Sparko." Any of the photos and historical documents can be zoomed in to for easy viewing of details; just spread two fingers apart on your iPad with the usual multi-touch gesture.

Audience

People of all ages who are interested in the 1939–40 New York World's Fair. Historians and scholars who want to see what's available in this wonderful, historic collection.

Other Apps Worth Trying

- NYPL Biblion: Frankenstein: The Afterlife of Shelley's Circle: http://exhibitions.nypl.org/biblion/outsiders. iOS (iPad only).

Viewing Rare Manuscripts

PictureIt: EP

- Developer: The University of Michigan, http://um3d.dc.umich.edu/portfolio/pictureit
- Version: 1.1
- Platforms: iOS (universal)
- Price: Free

This app showcases 30 pages of the world's oldest existing manuscript of the letters of St. Paul, dating from 180 to 220 AD, known as Papyrus 46.[2] You can view images of the pages in the original Greek, then tap on a small icon to open a viewer that translates it to English. The viewer is like a virtual magnifying glass that you drag down the page while reading, showing you the translation of a few lines at a time.

Tap another icon and the whole page switches to English. Tap it again to switch back to Greek with the translator tool. It's designed to give you a feel for reading an ancient Greek book on papyrus. Annotations explain how certain details of the translation differ from the New Testament translations that many are familiar with.

This project is from the University of Michigan 3D Lab. It's one of several projects designed to showcase rare books with an online interface for easy reading.

Audience

Scholars or anyone interested in viewing ancient manuscripts with the original Greek, plus translations.

Photo Exhibit with Walking Tour

WolfWalk

- Developer: NC State University, http://www.lib.ncsu.edu/wolfwalk/
- Version: 1.2.1
- Platforms: iOS (universal)
- Price: Free

This app is a photographic guide to the history of North Carolina State University, combined with a walking tour.[3] It includes more than 1,000 historical photographs, organized by place, decades, or themes.

This works especially well on the iPad, since the photographs can fill the screen and you can zoom on the details with multitouch gestures. If you are on the campus, a map will show you where you are and you can tap on the "i" button for particular campus locations to view the historical photos. Each photo has accompanying text that explains the context and history.

If you're not currently on campus when using the app, you can still browse the list of places alphabetically or by viewing them on a map. Decades range from pre-1900 to the 2000s. Themes include athletics, construction, events, long gone, people, residential life, student life, and teaching and research.

This app is a wonderful way to showcase historical photographs while taking advantage of the location awareness of mobile devices—resulting in an interesting walking tour app.

Audience

Anyone interested in the history of NC State University.

Other Apps Worth Trying

- Library of Congress—Virtual Tour: http://www.loc.gov/apps/. iOS.

Showcasing Exhibits

To the Brink: JFK and the Cuban Missile Crisis

- Developer: National Archives and Records Administration, http://foundationnationalarchives.org/cmc/, and http://www.archives.gov/social-media/mobile-apps.html

- Version: 1.1

- Platforms: iOS (iPad only)

- Price: Free

To the Brink is a well-designed app that showcases a 2013 exhibit about the Cuban Missile Crisis from the National Archives and the JFK Library. It's easy to browse—swipe to a section, read a summary, and then tap on icons to view a gallery of photos, historical documents, short videos, audio recordings, and more textual information.

Historical documents include declassified CIA documents—such as a personality sketch of Nikita Khrushchev, a psychiatric personality study of Fidel Castro, President Kennedy's doodle notes, and a reading copy of his address to the nation from October 22, 1962. Many more documents and photos give you a sense of what was happening at the time.

This app is a good example of how to bring exhibits to the public, making them a personal exploration for reading and viewing on the iPad. The simplicity and usability of this design could be used as a template or example for any exhibit from a library or historical archives.

Audience

Anyone interested in the Cuban Missile Crisis and also those interested in seeing a well-designed user interface for exhibit apps in order to plan one for their own institution.

Other Apps Worth Trying

- National Archives DocsTeach: http://docsteach.org/. Classroom activities based on documents from the National Archives. IOS (iPad only).

Notes

1. Details about NYPL Biblion: World's Fair: http://exhibitions.nypl.org/biblion/worldsfair.

2. http://www.annarbor.com/news/university-of-michigan-st-paul-ancient-letters-ipad/.

3. Press release for the iPad version of this app: http://news.lib.ncsu.edu/2011/06/16/ncsu-libraries-brings-photographic-history-of-nc-state-to-the-ipad/.

CHAPTER 11

Apps for Going Beyond the Library Catalog

Barcode Scanning

RedLaser

- Developer: eBay Inc., http://redlaser.com/
- Version: 5.0.1
- Platforms: Android, iOS
- Price: Free

RedLaser is a useful app for scanning barcodes of different types, from UPC codes to QR codes. It's designed for comparison shopping—when you're in a store, pick up a product with a barcode and scan it with this app. You'll see a list of online stores that carry the item, along with the price and reviews. You can add items you've scanned to lists of your own creation.

One thing that makes this useful for libraries is its connection to World-Cat.[1] If you scan the barcode of a book, it will show you the price in various online stores, and if you tap on the "local" tab, you'll see a list of WorldCat member libraries near you that have the book. When you tap on the name of a particular library, you'll see the address on a map, and if you tap "find book," it will link to the catalog of that library.

Figure 11.1: Link to a video about how to use barcode-scanning apps

Another interesting feature of this app is that it can create QR codes. These are square barcodes that are often seen on posters or magazine ads, and they can link you to a number of different things when you point your QR-reading app to the code. For example, a poster about a local music concert could have a QR code that links to the location on a map of the venue. Capture it with your mobile phone, using a QR code–reading app like this one, and the location will open immediately in the map on your phone.

QR codes can be created that link to a particular URL, a person's contact information, a text message, or a location on a map. To create a code with RedLaser, tap "home," then "QR codes," then select from the following: share URL, share my info, share a contact, share text, share my location. Fill in the info and you'll get a QR code that you can save to your camera roll or e-mail.

To give it a try, scan this QR code with Red Laser and you'll be taken to a video I created about how to use barcode-scanning apps.[2]

Audience
Anyone who would like to do comparison shopping, people who want to see if their local library has a book they see when browsing in a store, and anyone who wants to create and use QR codes.

Examples
QR codes are an interesting way to connect the print and digital worlds. Some libraries are putting QR codes on signs near their print journals, so people quickly connect to the e-journals for those titles. For an interesting discussion of QR codes in libraries, see "E-Discovery with QR Codes," by Meridith Farkas.[3]

For some interesting ideas for teachers and schools using QR codes, including treasure hunts, worksheets that link to videos, and more, see "Exploring the Educational Potential of QR Codes,"[4] by Joe Dale.

Other Apps Worth Trying

- Book Crawler: http://www.chiisai.com/. iOS (universal). Create a personal database of books by scanning their barcodes to enter them into your catalog.

- NeoReader: http://www.neoreader.com/. Android, iOS (universal). An excellent QR code reader app.

Kiosks

Kiosk Pro

- Developer: Kiosk Pro, http://www.kioskproapp.com/

- Version: 3.5.2

- Platforms: iOS (universal)

- Price: $4.99

If you would like to set up an iPad as an informational kiosk in your library, this is the app to use. There are several kiosk apps available, and this one is useful because of the large number of settings and customizations available.

With it, you can run files stored locally on the iPad, so that if the Internet connection goes down, your kiosk will still work. You can turn off the navigation of a page, so that it fills the screen. Create a custom web page with links to the information you want to provide and set it as the home screen on your kiosk. You can set a timer so that after a set period without use, it will return to the main screen.

Another useful feature is that you can create a list of allowed domains, limiting the sites that people can browse to. Many other features are available, such as allowing printing to AirPrint-enabled printers, auto-playing HTML5 audio or video, and saving form submissions locally on the iPad.

You can also monitor your kiosk remotely and even have it e-mail you if your kiosk loses power. To prevent users from exiting the app, you can use Apple's Guided Access mode to disable the "home" button.[5]

If you want to test this app before purchasing the pro edition, you can download Kiosk Pro Lite for free. If you're looking for a secure enclosure for your iPad kiosk, take a look at those available from http://www.ipadkiosks.com/.

Audience

Libraries, museums, and other institutions who want to set up kiosks for the public using iPads.

The MIT Libraries has installed an information kiosk on the second floor of one of their libraries. It features a secured iPad using Kiosk Pro that gives quick access to information on how to find books, the location of scanners/copies/printers, where to find food and drink, restroom locations, and more.[6]

Mobile Library Catalog

LibAnywhere

- Developer: LibraryThing, http://www.librarything.com/
- Version: 1.91
- Platforms: Android, iOS (universal)
- Price: Free

LibAnywhere is a mobile app for searching library catalogs of participating libraries. Published by LibraryThing.com, it allows you to select a library (or browse for nearby libraries), search the catalog, place holds, see what you have checked out, contact a librarian, and more, depending on what the particular library has set up. The app makes it easy for users to add particular items to a favorites list or scan a barcode with your mobile device's camera to see if your library has that title.

To learn more about how your library can get a custom-branded app with this service, see LibraryThing for Libraries at http://www.librarything .com/forlibraries/index.php?page=libanywhere and watch their video screencasts.[7]

Audience

Users of participating libraries who want to search their local catalogs on the go. Libraries who want an easy way to set up a mobile app for their catalogs.

Example

For a good example of how a public library is using this, see the Danbury Public Library[8] in Danbury, Connecticut. In the Library Anywhere app you can see their hours and locations, tap on the phone number to have your mobile phone call the number, tap on the Google maps link for directions, see their event listings, check your account, ask a librarian, and follow links to their Facebook page, eBooks catalog from 3M, Freegal catalog of music online, and link to their full website.

Other Apps Worth Trying

- Readar: https://itunes.apple.com/us/app/readar/id431326874?mt=8. iOS. LibraryThing's app for finding book-related events near you.

Augmented Reality

Layar—Augmented Reality

- Developer: Layar B.V., https://www.layar.com/products/app/
- Version: 8.1
- Platforms: Android, iOS (universal)
- Price: Free

Layar is what's known as an "augmented reality" app. It provides a way to view a live image of the physical world, with virtual images superimposed—designed to augment what you're seeing with useful information. To try it, look for items that have the Layar icon on them, such as magazine ads, posters, billboards, or business cards. Scan the item with your mobile phone using the Layar app and additional content will appear to be floating over the physical object.

If you don't have any of these objects nearby, you can try it by scanning some of the images provided for you by Layar on their Pinterest board at http://www.pinterest.com/Layar/layar-initiatives/. You can also scan cash that you have on hand, for a fun experience (U.S. dollars, Canadian dollars, euros, British pounds, Indian rupees, or Thai baht).[9]

For example, a movie poster when scanned might bring up a trailer of the movie, or a magazine ad might bring up a discount coupon for a product that you can save in your Layar app. It works best when you are on a Wi-Fi network or a fast cellular data connection, because the app needs to go online to find and show the digital content. You can also scan QR codes with Layar and you'll see a link to what the QR code points to, so you can tap and follow it.

There is also a feature called "geo layers." You can try this without needing to find a particular object to scan. Tap in the sidebar menu, select a category (such as Instagram photos, food and drink, tourism, or search), then point your camera anywhere and you will see the world around you with images floating above it that represent the items it finds. A listing for a restaurant shows the address, a photo, the distance from you, a link to their website, a link to reviews, and a link to directions in your mobile phone's mapping app. You can choose to view the floating items on a map (so you don't have to keep moving your phone around to see what's in different directions). Filters allow you to choose the distance away from you that you would like included in your search (up to 1.6 miles).

Layar keeps a list of everything you've viewed, so you can easily go back to maps, coupons, or other information. Layar also provides a tool for creating your own AR content. For more information, see https://www.layar.com/products/creator/.

If you don't have Layar but want to see how it works, see their video demo: http://youtu.be/MsMuKTkgw0k.

Audience

Anyone who wants to find interesting places around them while traveling, and also those who want to explore virtual reality in its current form.

Examples

Layar is just one example of an app that uses augmented reality. It's useful to try it so you can see what this technology can do.

Of possible interest to libraries are augmented reality books. Here's an example: *Horrible Hauntings: An Augmented Reality Collection of Ghosts and Ghouls.*[10] Buy a copy of the printed book, and then download a free copy of its companion app[11] (instead of Layar). Using the app, you'll see images of ghosts from each story appear to float off the page in the air in front of you. A demo video is available here: http://youtu.be /7SsYUQSTtok.

Augmented reality has many applications on the horizon for the near future, with technologies like Google Glass.[12] For a brief overview of applications, see "5 Augmented Reality Trends for 2014."[13]

Location-Based Check-Ins

Foursquare

- Developer: Foursquare Labs Inc., https://foursquare.com/
- Version: 7.0.1
- Platforms: Android, iOS
- Price: Free

Foursquare is a popular social network for sharing your current location with friends. With it, you can "check in" when you go to a restaurant, bookstore, or other location and your friends on Foursquare will see where you are. You can also leave tips about a location and read tips that others have posted, such as what's particularly good on the menu or what the Wi-Fi password is in your local cafe.

Open the app, tap the button, and it will show you a list of known local places. If your place is in the list, tap it and add a comment or tip, and add a photo, if you like. If your place is not in the list, you can search for it, and if you still don't find it, you can add it to the Foursquare database. You'll be asked to enter a name, a category (food, outdoors & recreation, residence, and so on), and an optional address. Then others will be able to check in to the location you've added.

Some venues offer special discounts or coupons that you can get when you visit their location and check in. You can also get gaming-style badges for having the most check-ins at particular locations (compete with your friends). There are badges for everything from cities, to expertise, to special events. For example, get the "bookworm" badge for checking in at a large number of bookstores,[14] or the "Sakura" badge for check-ins in Tokyo. Institutions can create badges—for example, you can earn the "Blue Devil" badge for check-ins at Duke University.[15]

You can also make lists of places with Foursquare and browse the lists that others have made. There are lists on many topics, for example, "The Best Museums in New York City"[16] or "Boston Public Libraries" (a list of each branch library).[17] You can save your favorite lists and make it a goal to check in at all the places on the list.

Foursquare is especially useful when you are traveling and visiting unfamiliar locations. It's a great way to get tips and recommendations on the best places to visit nearby. It's also a useful way for an institution to give tips about its venue and invite more people to visit, through entries on lists, giving special badges, and offering useful tips.

As of this writing, Foursquare has announced plans to split their app into two different apps. They will put the "check-in" features in an app called Swarm,[18] and then update Foursquare to focus on the recommendation features, rather than "check-ins."[19] This keeps the useful features for libraries in the main Foursquare app.

Audience

Anyone who enjoys sharing information about places they visit and learning about the places around them, especially while traveling or moving to a new city.

Examples

Libraries can use Foursquare to create a list of all their branches. See the Boston Public Library at https://foursquare.com/notifyboston/list/boston-public-libraries or the MIT Libraries at https://foursquare.com/mitlibraries/list/mit-library-locations.

Foursquare users (including library staff) can leave tips about specific items in the libraries on Foursquare. These will show when someone checks in with the app. The Boston Public Library has tips about their art and architecture tour, best places to study, and more; see: http://4sq.com/2oNOFF.

Crowdfunding

Kickstarter

- Developer: Kickstarter Inc., http://www.kickstarter.com/mobile
- Version: 1.4.1
- Platforms: Android, iOS
- Price: Free

Kickstarter is a way to fund creative projects, known as "crowdfunding." Post a video about your idea, set a funding amount goal, and post your project to Kickstarter, allowing individuals to back your project by donating money. If you meet your funding goal in the allotted time period, Kickstarter will charge all the backers and you have your funds; if you don't meet the goal, no one gets charged.

It is customary to set up rewards of various types for different funding amounts and the backers receive them if the project meets its funding goal. For example, backers of the film *The Wireless Generation*[20] received a mention on the film's official website for a $5 donation, an HD digital download of the entire film before the official release for a $25 donation, a DVD with special features (and all other lower rewards) for $50 or more, a private screening of the film in their city for $2,500 or more, and for $5,000 or more, "executive producer" credit in IMDb with an invitation to attend special VIP events for the film (in addition to all previous level rewards).

Types of projects that can be posted on Kickstarter include: art, comics, dance, design, fashion, film, food, games, music, photography, publishing, technology, and theater. Each project needs a clear goal, such as creating a work of art or writing a book.

The Kickstarter mobile app is a great way to browse projects and decide which ones to back. Browse staff picks, popular, nearby (using location awareness of your mobile phone), and starred (your favorites). Watch videos made by the creators explaining their projects and choose which ones to back. After entering your funding amount, the app uses Amazon payments to complete your donation. You won't be charged unless the project meets its goal. You can also send links to spread the word about your favorite projects on Twitter, Facebook, or e-mail.

It's also a great way to keep tabs on your own Kickstarter project and see how close you are to reaching your funding goal. Stay connected with your backers by posting project updates.

Audience

Anyone who has a creative project that needs funding and wants to keep up with how close they are to meeting their funding goals. Also great for browsing and donating to other projects and getting inspired with ideas for creative projects that your library could submit.

Examples

Libraries are using Kickstarter to raise funding for all sorts of interesting projects. Here are just a few examples:

1. Little Free Library Project: Winston-Salem, North Carolina. Take a book, leave a book, in small kiosks.
https://www.kickstarter.com/projects/1106918453/little-free-library -project-winston-salem-nc.

2. Library for All: A Digital Library for the Developing World. Building a digital platform for low-cost access to a digital library that can be used on mobile phones, low-cost tablets, and e-readers.
https://www.kickstarter.com/projects/1692978335/library-for-all-a -digital-library-for-the-developi.

3. "I matter" Project at Northport Public Library. A project allowing teens to express themselves through large-format photographs and "I matter" statements.
https://www.kickstarter.com/projects/2083339466/i-matter-project -at-northport-public-library.

4. Circulating Ideas: The Librarian Interview Podcast. A project to expand the podcast of interviews with librarians, showcasing the innovative work they are doing.
https://www.kickstarter.com/projects/201101936/circulating-ideas -the-librarian-interview-podcast.

Notes

1. RedLaser iPhone app adds library listings through WorldCat APIs: http://www.oclc.org/developer/news/2010/redlaser-iphone-app-adds-library-listings -through-worldcat-apis.en.html.
2. Or just watch this demo video if you don't have a QR code reader: http://youtu.be/MQpaTgMTrQg.
3. http://www.americanlibrariesmagazine.org/article/e-discovery-qr-codes.
4. http://connectlearningtoday.com/exploring-the-educational-potential-of-qr -codes-3/.
5. How to use guided access to disable the "home" button: http://support.apple.com/kb/ht5509.
6. "New 'Find It' Information Kiosk Unveiled at Hayden Library": http://libraries.mit.edu/news/find-information-kiosk/9069/.
7. Library Anywhere screencasts: http://www.librarything.com/forlibraries/video_la.php.
8. Danbury Public Library: http://www.danburylibrary.org/.
9. Scan your cash with Layar: https://www.layar.com/news/blog/2013/09/19/scan-money-with-layar/.

10. *Horrible Hauntings: An Augmented Reality Collection of Ghosts and Ghouls*, published by Goosebottom Books: http://goosebottombooks.com/home/pages/OurBooksDetail/horrible-hauntings.

11. Horrible Hauntings companion app: https://itunes.apple.com/us/app/horrible-hauntings/id553381348?mt=8.

12. Watch these videos from the Google Glass explorer program to see how it works: http://www.google.com/glass/start/explorer-stories/.

13. "5 Augmented Reality Trends for 2014": http://www.hhglobal.com/blog/5-augmented-reality-trends-for-2014.

14. Foursquare badges: http://aboutfoursquare.com/foursquare-badge-list/foursquare-badges/.

15. College and university badges on Foursquare: http://aboutfoursquare.com/foursquare-badge-list/partner-badges/college-badges/.

16. Foursquare list example, Best Museums in New York City: https://foursquare.com/corcoran_group/list/best-museums-in-new-york-city.

17. Foursquare list example, Boston Public Libraries: https://foursquare.com/notifyboston/list/boston-public-libraries.

18. Swarm: https://itunes.apple.com/us/app/swarm-by-foursquare/id870161082?mt=8.

19. http://www.theverge.com/2014/5/1/5666062/foursquare-swarm-new-app.

20. The Wireless Generation project on Kickstarter: https://www.kickstarter.com/projects/almostfearless/the-wireless-generation.

CHAPTER 12

Apps for Professional Development

Resume Creation

ResumeBase

- Developer: Abovehorizon, http://www.resumebase.net/
- Version: 1.3
- Platforms: iOS (iPad only)
- Price: $2.99

ResumeBase helps you create multiple versions of your resume. It stores each bit of information in a database from which you can draw information when you create a particular resume.

Input all of your information, then select either a chronological or a functional resume. From there you can build your resume by selecting the details you want to include. When you're done, you can view it, print it, or e-mail it to yourself for further customization using your computer. You can also open a plain-text version that can be opened and edited in other apps on your iPad.

Keep notes within the app for each version of your resume, such as what position it was used for and who you sent it to. You can keep updating your information in the app and use it to make new versions of your resume over time.

Audience

Job seekers who want to easily create and update their resume on the iPad.

Other Apps Worth Trying

- Resume Builder Pro: https://itunes.apple.com/us/app/pocket-resume/id365420856?mt=8&ign-mpt=uo%3D4. Android, iOS (universal). Another well-reviewed resume creation app.

- Templates for Pages: https://itunes.apple.com/us/app/templates-for-pages-for-ipad/id442548006?mt=8. iOS (universal). Apple's Pages app (described elsewhere in this book) has templates available for making nicely designed resumes.

Creating Your Personal Social Site and Making Connections with Colleagues

About.me

- Developer: about.me https://about.me/
- Version: 2.1.1
- Platforms: iOS
- Price: Free; pro accounts available for $4/month

About.me is a website that makes it easy for you to create a professional profile that links to all of your social networks. Upload a photo, select a background and other styling elements, write a brief description of yourself, and link to your social networks, such as Twitter, Facebook, Instagram, and more.

Once you're in About.me, you can use the mobile app to browse for others who have similar interests or who are following you on Twitter. It's a good way to find out more about your Twitter followers and make connections with people of common interests.

You can create collections of people using the app. Tap on someone's profile, select "add to collection," then select "Twitter friends," "complimented me," or "start a new collection." The compliment feature is a nice way to show someone you like their profile; it's similar to the "like" button on Facebook. When you tap the "compliment" button, you can choose from options such as "add to favorites," "love your page," "great photo," "awesome bio," "you're cool," "I'm a fan," or "creative."

To find interesting people, browse through lists of people who have "things in common with me," "shares my interests," "shares my location," "complimented me," "added me to a collection," "viewed my page," "Twitter followers," "Instagram followers," "LinkedIn connections," and more.

All of these features are available with a free account. Pro accounts ($4/month) add the ability to use a custom domain, remove all about.me branding, add Google Analytics, and get priority support.

Audience

Anyone who would like an easy way to create a web presence that offers brief information about themselves with links to their social media profiles and resume. People wishing to network with others of similar interests.

Examples

To find librarians on About.me, search for "librarian" or "librarians"— http://about.me/search/keyword:librarian, http://about.me/search/keyword:librarians. Here are a few individual examples: The Natural Librarian: http://about.me/thenaturallibrarian, Steven R. Harris: http://about.me/srharris19, Greg Hardin: http://about.me/ghardin, and Nicole Hennig: http://about.me/nic221/.

Searching for Jobs

Job Search by Indeed.com

- Developer: Indeed.com, http://www.indeed.com/
- Version: 2.3
- Platforms: Android, iOS (universal)
- Price: Free

Indeed.com is one of the largest search engines for job listings. The mobile app makes it easy to search the listings, read the detailed job descriptions, save them to a favorites list, forward listings by e-mail, and learn more about particular employers by reading their ratings and reviews.

The search feature works well—you can enter keywords, choose a location (or nationwide), filter by distance from the location you entered, and sort by relevance or date. You can search listings in more than 50 countries and 28 languages.

You can follow your favorite companies or employers by searching for one, then tapping "be the first to see new jobs." The app will then e-mail you with updates when new jobs from that employer are posted.

Tip: if you are looking for jobs that can be done from home, or from any geographic location, search for the keyword, "remote."

If you sign up for a free account, you can post your resume on the site and apply from directly within the app.

Audience
Job seekers who want an easy way to search for and manage job listings.

Job Searching and Networking

LinkedIn

- Developer: LinkedIn Corporation, http://www.linkedin.com/mobile
- Version: 7.0.3
- Platforms: Android, iOS (universal)
- Price: Free; premium accounts available

The LinkedIn mobile app is a good way to keep up with LinkedIn on the go. Use it to search for a person you are going to meet with, accept connections, browse recommended jobs, see updates from groups you are a member of, and more.

You can add connections, reply to or compose individual messages, post updates, and read updates in your stream. A feature called "Pulse" lets you create and browse a custom newsfeed with stories in categories you can select, such as "professional women," "higher education," "big ideas and innovation," or "technology."

You can also update your own profile with the app, including uploading a new photo directly from your phone. If you are browsing the jobs section, you can save the jobs you are interested in to a list called "your saved jobs."

If you upgrade from a free to a premium account you get the following:

- See everyone who has viewed your profile in the last 90 days.
- See full profiles of everyone in your network.
- Send direct messages to anyone on LinkedIn.
- Use the premium search engine with advanced filters and alerts.

Different levels of premium accounts are available from $24.99 per month to $99.99 per month.[1]

Audience

Job seekers and anyone who wants to network with their professional colleagues.

Examples

If you would like to join groups on LinkedIn, you can start by searching for professional associations, schools you have attended, or groups formed around special interests. Here are a few examples.

- ASIS&T: http://www.linkedin.com/groups/Association-Information -Science-Technology-44332?gid=44332.

- LIS Career Options, a subgroup of ALA: http://www.linkedin.com/ groups?home=&gid=3126663.

- Librarian Alternatives: http://www.linkedin.com/groups/Librarian -Alternatives-2244928.

- Librarians in the Job Market: http://www.linkedin.com/groups/ Librarians-In-Job-Market-3023932.

- Simmons GSLIS Alumni: http://www.linkedin.com/groups? home=&gid=103176.

Conferences

Lanyrd

- Developer: Eventbrite, http://lanyrd.com/mobile/
- Version: 3.0.0
- Platforms: Android, iOS (universal)
- Price: Free

Lanyrd is an app for tracking information about conferences. You can use it to find events of possible interest, see who else is attending and speaking, keep track of your own conference attendance and speaking history, and more.

Sign up for a free account to use it, and if you would like to see which conferences the people you follow are attending, you can connect your Twitter and LinkedIn profiles.

Anyone can add events to Lanyrd, similar to how Wikipedia works. According to Lanyrd's FAQ, they have a way of removing vandalism and false entries from the site.[2] If you are planning an event, create an entry in the web version (Lanyrd.com) and others will be able to follow it and track it. Events can be conferences, workshops, meetups, "un-conferences"—any kind of event.[3]

You can use the app to search for a particular event or for events on a topic. Currently, there are not a large number of library-related events in Lanyrd, though there are some. If you are planning an event and want to publicize it, listing it in Lanyrd is a good way to start. In addition to the usual dates, location, and summary, you can enter the conference hashtag, link to the conference website, provide links to registration, and more.

In the mobile app, you can view your profile, set your messaging preferences (such as who is allowed to message you in the app), and see a list of your events. The list includes events you've marked as "attending" and events you've marked as "tracking." Tracking is a useful way to follow events that you are interested in but may not be able to attend. You'll get updates and links to the conference materials that have been posted after the event, and see the hashtags, in case you would like to follow the live tweets. You can also see past events that you've attended, spoken at, or tracked.

You can also "discover" events, which shows you lists of suggested events similar to the ones you've already attended, by matching keywords and by showing events that your friends and followers from LinkedIn or Twitter are attending or tracking.

For each event description, topical keywords can be assigned. This makes it easy to find similar events that might interest you. If you enjoy a particular speaker, you can follow links to their profile on Lanyard and see what other events they are speaking at. You can "track" people who are speakers as well, which gives you a list of their speaking events and other useful information. You can even tap the "want to meet" button and the "introduce yourself" button as a way to network with people through the app.

If you speak at conferences, you can set up your profile using the web version of the app, and link to your slide decks, blog posts, and other related material, including links to books you've written. Lanyrd has a speaking directory (http://lanyrd.com/speakers/), and your entry will appear in it when people are searching for possible speakers.

See their helpful FAQ for more information about Lanyrd: http://lanyrd.com/help/faq/.

Audience
Anyone who attends or speaks at conferences and wants a handy way to find and track events and people they meet.

Here's an example of a small conference related to libraries: Innovation, Inspiration, and Creativity Conference, http://lanyrd.com/2014/i2c2/; and a large technology conference that librarians sometimes attend: SXSW Interactive 2014, http://lanyrd.com/2014/sxsw-interactive/.

Scan and Save Business Cards

Evernote Hello

- Developer: Evernote, http://evernote.com/hello/
- Version: 2.2.2
- Platforms: Android, iOS
- Price: Free

Evernote Hello is designed to help you remember everyone you meet and keep a record of your meetings with them. There are three ways to enter information: scan a business card, type in a name or e-mail address, or use "Hello Connect," which scans the environment for others nearby who also have the app and agree to share their information. That's a nice feature when you are with a group of people who all have the app and want to add each other's contact information all at once.[4]

If you choose to scan a card, hold the iPhone at an angle where you can see the card. The app will capture the photo and flatten it automatically. It will add all the information that it recognizes from the image (you can edit if it makes any errors in the recognition). It will save the information in the app and also synchronize it with your Evernote account, where you can tell it to sync with the notebook of your choice. You can also choose to automatically save people to your iPhone contacts.

If you opt to connect the app to LinkedIn and/or Facebook, it will find and add information from those sources to your scanned contact information. You can make notes about when you met the person and anything you would like to record about the meeting. It keeps all the information in a timeline, allowing you to scroll back and see all the people you've met.

The app is a handy way to turn all those physical cards that you get from people into digital information, saved in Evernote.

Audience

Anyone who collects business cards from others and would like an easy way to enter them into Evernote and/or their contacts app on the iPhone.

Other Apps Worth Trying

These apps have also received favorable reviews.

- ScanBizCards: https://www.circleback.com/scanbizcards/. Android, iOS.

- WorldCard Mobile Lite: http://worldcard.penpowerinc.com/product.asp?sn=158. Android, iOS.

- CamCard Free: https://play.google.com/store/apps/details?id=com.intsig.BCRLite&feature=search_result. Android.

Attending Webinars

Cisco WebEx Meetings

- Developer: Cisco, http://www.webex.com/products/web-conferencing/mobile.html

- Version: 5.0

- Platforms: Android, iOS (universal)

- Price: Free

If you attend webinars or meetings powered by WebEx, you'll find the mobile app handy. With it you can join a meeting by meeting number or by logging in to your WebEx account.

With the mobile app, you can schedule, host, or attend meetings. The app uses your phone's video camera to provide your image if your meeting is a video-based meeting. As an attendee, you can view the slides, see a video of the presenter (if they are making it available), hear the audio, and participate in private or group chat.

The app works over Wi-Fi, 3G/4G, and LTE, so you can watch from anywhere you have online access. You can view shared content with annotations, see the attendee list, and pinch to zoom in for a close-up view.

Learn more about the WebEx mobile apps, which are available on multiple platforms: http://www.webex.com/products/web-conferencing/mobile.html.

Audience

Anyone who wants to attend webinars while away from their computer or get convenient mobile access to remote meetings.

Other Apps Worth Trying

- Adobe Connect Mobile: http://www.adobe.com/products/adobeconnect/mobile-meetings.html. Android, iOS (universal).

Notes

1. LinkedIn premium accounts: http://premium.linkedin.com/.
2. Lanyrd's FAQ: http://lanyrd.com/help/faq/.
3. If you're not familiar with unconferences, try one—they are fun and useful! See http://en.wikipedia.org/wiki/Unconference.
4. The Evernote Hello website has some useful videos showing how these features work: http://evernote.com/hello/.

CHAPTER 13

Element of App-Literacy

Apple's iOS Human Interface Guidelines

Apple publishes detailed guidelines to guide app developers when designing their apps. It's worthwhile to read some of these, even if you aren't a developer, because you'll learn the principles of creating a good user experience. This will help you when evaluating and reviewing apps.

For example, if you are reviewing an app and you fault the app for not providing extensive onscreen help, you'll be wrong, because Apple encourages developers to make apps so easy that they don't require a lot of help screens.

The guidelines are available for free on Apple's develop website.[1]

iOS 7 Human Interface Guidelines[2]

The following sections are recommended reading if you are not a developer but want to understand why and how Apple's user experience is so carefully designed. This is especially useful if you will be writing reviews of apps. Look for the most current version of iOS human interface guidelines, such as iOS 8, or the most current one at the time you are reading this.

UI Design Basics
- Starting and stopping
- Interactivity and feedback

- Branding
- Color and typography
- Terminology and wording

Design Strategies
- Design principles

iOS Technologies
- Multitasking

- Social media

- iCloud

- Notification center

- Location services

- Sound

- VoiceOver

Icon and Image Design
- App icon

There are many more sections, but those listed above are an excellent starting point.

If you'd like to learn more about how to design great iOS apps, read William Van Hecke's *Learning iOS Design: A Hands-On Guide for Programmers and Designers.*[3]

This is helpful even if you're outsourcing app design. It will help you understand what to include in your specifications if you're working on an app project for your library or institution.

Mobile Device Capabilities

Another important aspect of app-literacy is developing an understanding of how apps take advantage of the capabilities of mobile devices.

For example, the app *Leafsnap: An Electronic Field Guide*[4] uses the built-in camera to identify tree species from photos of their leaves. You can snap a photo of a leaf with your mobile device's camera, and the app will identify it by shape, linking you to a detailed entry with more information. It uses geolocation to show you where you are on a map and link you to the descriptions of the types of trees that are nearby.

Leafsnap was developed by researchers from Columbia University, the University of Maryland, and the Smithsonian Institution. Their goal is to turn app users into citizen scientists, sharing data with a community of scientists who will map and monitor the ebb and flow of flora throughout the United States.

This is just one example of what mobile apps can do that is different from what desktops and laptops can do.

Important Mobile Device Features

Here's a list of some important features that are available in most smart-phones and tablets.

If you are reviewing and evaluating apps, it's good to discuss how the app makes use of these features.

1. Front and rear cameras (still and video): The cameras in mobile devices are used not only for photography but also for live video conversations with Skype or FaceTime,[5] mobile scanning apps, such as JotNot Scanner Pro,[6] and barcode-scanning apps, such as Red Laser.[7]

2. Built-in microphone: This is used not only for phone conversations but also for apps that use speech recognition, such as Dragon Dictation, which translates your voice to text. It's also used for apps that recognize music that is playing around you, like SoundHound.[8]

3. Built-in speakers and headphone jacks: Having sound output is useful both for the built-in speaker and also for using external speakers. It's possible to connect in several ways: wire from headphone jack to external speakers, Bluetooth wireless speakers (see Bluetooth connectivity, below), or Apple's AirPlay feature,[9] which allows streaming audio and video out to Apple TV, Apple's Airport Express (which itself could be plugged into a speaker system), or AirPlay-enabled speakers.

4. Accelerometer: The accelerometer measures the force of acceleration, whether caused by gravity or by movement. This allows your device to sense which way the screen is being held so it can adjust the orientation. This is used when you want to watch a video or read an eBook in either landscape or portrait. It's also used in many games.

5. Gyroscope: A three-axis gyroscope, paired with the accelerometer, makes a device capable of advanced motion sensing. It allows the device to sense how far, how fast, and in which direction it has moved in space. It's most often used in augmented reality apps, games, and photography apps (for panoramic photos).[10]

6. Compass: The iPhone's digital compass technology tells you which way the iPhone is facing in real time. It's used in map apps, compass apps, and specialized apps, such as astronomy apps[11] that show constellation information superimposed on the night sky.

7. Location awareness: This technology delivers information about your device's physical location to other users or apps. A device's location is usually determined by one of three methods: by GPS satellite tracking, by cell tower triangulation, or by the device's address on a Wi-Fi network. This is how the maps apps and many other apps can both show where you are and tailor information to your location (such as nearby tweets).

8. Touch screen: A touch screen display allows user control by touching the screen with one or more fingers. It allows direct interaction with what's on the screen, rather than using a mouse, trackpad, or other pointing device. Multi-touch screens can recognize the presence of two or more points of contact with the surface. This allows for easy control by pinching, zooming, long press, and other gestures.[12]

9. Data storage: Mobile devices either come with a fixed amount of data storage or are expandable, usually with microSD memory cards. Apple's devices are fixed, usually 16 GB, 32 GB, 64 GB, or 128 GB. Higher capacity allows for storing more movies, music, and other large files. Some interactive book apps, for example, take a lot of storage space for their multimedia features.

10. Wi-Fi and cellular connectivity: Wi-Fi is standard on smartphones and tablets. Smartphones use cellular networks by default. For tablets, if you want to be able to connect to the Internet using networks such as those from AT&T, Sprint, T-Mobile, or Verizon, you'll need a model that includes cellular capabilities, such as 3G, 4G, or LTE. iPads with this feature are contract-free, allowing you to pay only for the months in which you use the cellular service. Android tablets are sometimes sold with contracts, in a similar way to smartphones.

11. Bluetooth connectivity: Bluetooth is a wireless technology standard for exchanging data over short distances using radio waves. It's a very convenient way for devices to connect without wires, such as between your tablet and a wireless keyboard, or your smartphone and a wireless speaker.

12. NFC (Near Field Communication): This is a set of standards that allows for devices to establish radio communication with each other by touching them together or bringing them into close proximity. As of this writing, the technology is available in many Android devices but not those from Apple. It's commonly used for mobile payment systems, where you touch or wave your smartphone over an

NFC-enabled pay terminal. Google Wallet uses this technology. It's also available in San Francisco parking meters.

The more experience you have working with a wide range of apps, the more you will understand why tablets and smartphones are different types of devices from desktops and laptops. They are not just a poor, smaller-screened imitation of a laptop, but a complementary and unique device.

Jailbreaking: What Librarians Should Know

Even though the word "jailbreaking" sounds scary and illegal, it's not (on smartphones). Here is what you need to know:

- Jailbreaking allows you to install third-party apps from non-Apple stores, such as Cydia. (This is not the same as "unlocking," which means changing your smartphone to allow it to work on multiple carriers.)

- As of this writing, it's legal for smartphones but not tablets.[13] In 2010, the Copyright Office of the Library of Congress deemed that it's fair use to do this. These rules get reviewed every three years, and in 2012, they updated the ruling to exclude tablets. So as of 2012, it's not legal to jailbreak your iPad.[14] These rulings are something to watch, since they are reviewed every three years.

- If you jailbreak, there are some very useful apps[15] available that add functionality, such as turning your iPhone into a mobile Wi-Fi hotspot, for no extra charge other than the one-time cost of the app.

- It's fairly easy to do, and if anything goes wrong, you can easily restore your iPhone to its factory settings by resetting it in iTunes and restoring your files and apps from a backup.

Since the information on how to jailbreak changes with each update, it's recommended to search for the latest information at the time you decide to try jailbreaking. Search for "how to jailbreak an iPhone," or something similar. Find the newest articles from trusted sources, like Macworld.[16]

- Be aware that doing this will make your phone a bit more geeky and less user-friendly, since it adds more options, with some ugly settings screens, and so on.

- Whenever Apple comes out with an updated version of iOS, you won't be able to update your phone until there is a jailbreak for the new version. This can be from a few weeks to a couple of months later. So you may not be able to benefit from certain fixes or new features right away.

- Like most things, jailbreaking is a trade-off. You get a wide choice of useful apps, but you need to be a bit more of a techie and have the patience to deal with some not so user-friendly interfaces for finding and installing jailbroken apps.

Even if you have no desire to jailbreak your iPhone, it's good to be aware of what's possible and why people do it. If you or someone on your staff has this experience, you can recommend the best apps and tools to a user who is interested in doing this and has a need for a specialized app that's available only on Cydia.[17]

Apple's Accessibility Features for Mobile Devices

Apple's iOS is known for design that includes many excellent accessibility features that help with vision, hearing, physical motor skills, and learning/literacy.

Here is a list of those features. For details, see Apple's accessibility site.[18]

- VoiceOver
- Siri
- Speak Selection
- Dictation
- Zoom
- Large Text
- Invert Colors
- Braille Displays for iOS
- FaceTime
- Closed Captions
- Messages with iMessage
- Mono Audio
- Visible and Vibrating Alerts
- Made for iPhone Hearing Aids
- Assistive Touch
- Dictation
- Keyboard Shortcuts

- Guided Access
- Dictionary
- Safari Reader

These features are working out so well for users with disabilities that we're seeing inspiring examples in articles like these:

- "Re-Enabled: iOS's Impact on Those with Impairments Isn't Just a Marketing Slide; It's Profound"[19] by Steve Aquino.
- "How the Blind Are Reinventing the iPhone"[20] by Liat Kornowski.

Both articles frame the iPhone as a revolutionary development for people with disabilities. They discuss using Guided Access as a way to keep kids on task, and talk about how students are more attentive and engaged with course materials when using an iPad.

I encourage everyone to explore these features, because they are useful in many situations, whether you have a disability or not. Turning on Zoom is one of the first things I do whenever I get a new iPhone or iPad. It allows you to zoom in on any part of any screen, inside of any app. Very useful![21]

Reviewing Apps: A Checklist

It's becoming more common for librarians to review mobile apps for professional publications and blogs.

Here's a checklist I've developed as a guideline to reviewing mobile apps. This focuses on what you need to include that is specific to mobile apps. It can be used as a supplement to more general guidelines for writing reviews of books and other media.[22]

Header of review
- Your name and affiliation or expertise.
- App name: Check the app stores for official name, spelling and capitalization.
- App version.
- Developer, with link to their website's page about the app.
- Link to app stores (optional—because the developer's websites will have links to the app stores).
- Platforms (iOS, Android, web, other).
- If it's iOS, state whether it's a universal app, iPad only, or whether there are separate versions for iPhone and iPad.
- Price. Is there is a free version available? Are in-app purchases available?

Body of review

- Basic functionality: What exactly is it designed to do?
- Audience: Who is the app designed for? What age groups? (if appropriate) Who else might like to use it and why?
- Simplicity and ease of use: Can you figure out how to use it quickly? Can you use it in short bursts between other tasks? (a reality of mobile app usage)
- Playfulness: Does it delight the user? Is it fun to use?
- Visual design: Is it visually appealing? Is the icon distinctive and eye-catching?
- Sound design: If sound is included, do the sounds help you use the app? Are they of good quality? Are they customizable?
- How does the app work for users with disabilities? Does it have features that help those with low vision, hearing impairments, or other disabilities? If not, does the operation system provide for this? Apple's iOS is particularly good for accessibility features.[23]
- Examples: Give specific examples of how this app might be used.
- Related and similar apps: How does this app compare to other apps that do the same thing?

If appropriate, depending on the type of app, discuss the following.

- Does it work with bookmarking and storage services? (Instapaper, Pocket, Dropbox, iCloud, Google Drive)
- Can you sync information in the app between different devices? (smartphone, tablet, web version, desktop version)
- Can you easily share information from it on social networks? (Facebook, Twitter, Google+)
- Can you export to a variety of formats? (text, CSV, PDF, other)
- Can you import from a variety of media types? (text, videos, images, audio)
- Can selected material be copied and pasted elsewhere?
- Does it keep a history? (Example: Wikipedia apps often contain a useful history of items you've searched for).
- Does it have a wish list or favorites list so you can get back to your favorite items?
- Does it promote creative and imaginative uses?
- Does it provide for collaboration?
- Does it allow you to do something you were unable to do before you got the app?
- Does it allow you to do something that can't be done (or easily done) on a laptop or desktop computer? Specifically, how does it take advantage of the features of the mobile device, such as geo-location, camera, or accelerometer?
- Does it give you feedback? (quizzes, points, levels)
- Does it allow for personalization?

- Does it allow you to easily connect to information from outside the app? (with an in-app browser, or other feature)

Be sure to spell and capitalize the following words correctly:
- iOS
- iPad
- iPhone
- iPod Touch (not iTouch)
- apps (not APPS—it's not an acronym)

Watch out for auto-correction that will capitalize the lowercase "i" when you don't mean to.

I'd like to encourage librarians to review apps—both in the app stores and in your own sources of professional reading, such as journals and blogs. A good example of what librarians can do is seen in this crowd-sourced, professional network of librarians on the site Little eLit: Young Children, New Media, and Libraries at http://littleelit.com/. They have a section of their site devoted to apps, app reviews, and evaluating apps: http://littleelit.com/app-lists-reviews/. This group of librarians keeps an informative list of apps discussed on their site, with capsule reviews: http://littleelit.com/app-lists-reviews/apps-discussed-on-little-elit/. Librarians in many specific topic areas could create app review sites such as this one.[24]

We can help our communities, just as we always have with reviewing and selecting books and all kinds of multimedia materials. With so many apps available, more quality app reviews are needed!

Notes

1. iOS Design Resources: https://developer.apple.com/library/ios/design/index.html#/apple_ref/doc/uid/TP40013289.
2. Apple's iOS 7 Human Interface Guidelines: https://developer.apple.com/library/ios/documentation/UserExperience/Conceptual/MobileHIG/index.html#/apple_ref/doc/uid/TP40006556-CH66-SW1. Look for the most current version of iOS human interface guidelines, such as iOS 8, or the most current one at the time you are reading this.
3. "Learning iOS Design: A Hands-On Guide for Programmers and Designers": http://www.worldcat.org/oclc/854566942.
4. Leafsnap: An Electronic Field Guide: http://leafsnap.com/.
5. Apple's Facetime: http://www.apple.com/ios/facetime/.
6. JotNot Scanner Pro: http://www.mobitech3000.com/applications.html /.
7. Red Laser: http://redlaser.com/.
8. SoundHound: http://www.soundhound.com/.
9. AirPlay: https://www.apple.com/airplay/.

10. Here's a list of apps that use this feature: "Gyroscope Apps & Games" at http://www.phonearena.com/news/Gyroscope-apps-and-games_id15299.

11. Here's a list of stargazing apps (many make use of the compass): http://appadvice.com/appguides/show/astronomy-apps.

12. There is a list of these gestures, with video demonstrations, in this Wikipedia article: http://en.wikipedia.org/wiki/Multi-touch_gestures#Multi-touch_gestures.

13. The reasoning for this is that the word "tablet" was considered to be too ill-defined to allow the exception. People might interpret that one is allowed to jailbreak portable gaming consoles, e-readers, and laptops. See http://www.cultofmac.com/198298/new-copyright-office-ruling-allows-you-to-legally-jailbreak-your-iphone-but-not-your-ipad/.

14. The ruling (PDF): https://www.eff.org/files/filenode/dmca_2009/RM-2008-8.pdf.

15. Lifehacker has a good article recommending some of the best jailbreak apps:http://www.cultofmac.com/214983/here-are-the-very-best-jailbreak-tweaks-for-the-iphone-5-roundup/. Look for a newer version of this article that matches your iOS version at the time you read this.

16. "How to Jailbreak Your iPhone": http://www.macworld.com/article/2028546/how-to-jailbreak-your-iphone.html.

17. To learn more about the Cydia store, read this post from Lifehacker: http://lifehacker.com/5911486/im-new-to-jailbreaking-can-you-help-me-wrap-my-head-around-cydia.

18. iOS Accessibility features: http://www.apple.com/accessibility/ios/.

19. "Re-Enabled: iOS's Impact on Those with Impairments Isn't Just a Marketing Slide; It's Profound": http://the-magazine.org/9/re-enabled.

20. "How the Blind Are Reinventing the iPhone" by Liat Kornowski: http://www.theatlantic.com/technology/archive/2012/05/how-the-blind-are-reinventing-the-iphone/256589/.

21. "How to Zoom the Entire Screen on Your Smartphone or Tablet": http://www.techsupportalert.com/content/how-zoom-entire-screen-your-smartphone-or-tablet.htm.

22. For general guideline for writing reviews, see the ALA/RUSA CODES Materials Reviewing Committee, "Elements for Basic Reviews: A Guide for Writers and Readers of Reviews of Works in All Mediums and Genres," April 2005, http://www.ala.org/rusa/sites/ala.org.rusa/files/content/resources/guidelines/ElementsforReviews.pdf.

23. iOS Accessibility features: http://www.apple.com/accessibility/ios/.

24. Thanks to Angela Reynolds for recommending this site: http://littleelit.com/.

Further Resources

Ideas for Using Mobile Apps in Your Library

As you've seen throughout this book, there are many possibilities for using apps in creative ways in libraries. In my online course, "The Book as iPad App,"[1] one of the assignments is to participate in a virtual brainstorming activity using a shared document on Google Drive. Librarians in my course are from many types of libraries and this list is a summary of some of the ideas they came up with.

Since this course was focused on a particular type of app (interactive book apps), the ideas are mostly about those. Feel free to imagine using all the types of apps discussed in this book.

Events, Programs, and Instruction

- Use iPads for story time using interactive picture book apps. Pair up caregivers and kids to read together or project the app on a big screen. Have events where teens read to the young kids with iPad apps.

- Introduce graphic novels, both print and for iPad; do a presentation about them with iPad and projector.

- Have an app share event—everyone shares apps that have been helpful to them in daily life. Librarians provide a list of apps to start with. Call this "Appy Hour."

- Have classes for parents on the best iPad apps for kids of different age levels.

- Hold info sessions on interactive book apps to show people what's available.

- Have open sessions for playing with iPads (loaded with excellent content).

- Book app showcase—the library is a place to try out book apps before you buy them.

- Host app clubs—like book clubs, but for apps.

- Create presentations for specific departments at your university about the best apps for their field.[2]

- Invite the author of an interactive book app to come and give a presentation.

- Use an interactive book app as one of the books discussed in a traditional book club. Make it available to members on iPads they can borrow from the library or use in the library.

- Organize reviewing clubs for children and teens. iPads loaded with apps could be shared and the kids would rate and review them—and publish their reviews in a local newsletter.

- Create outreach programs for residents of nursing homes. Use content creation apps where seniors can tell their life story and interviews can be captured. Do presentations about specific times in history, using apps about the topic.

- Offer a session on apps for job searching and networking.

- Have instruction and liaison librarians explore and review apps that are relevant to their departments and subject areas. Create a display (online or offline) with images, descriptions, and links to the apps.

- Include apps in recommended lists of resources for students.

- Provide specialized instruction sessions using specific apps.

- Offer technology training for library staff: introduction to the best apps for your work and in different topic areas.

- Invite local artists, musicians, photographers, and writers who use apps to demonstrate what they do and which apps they use.

Content Creation and Publishing

- Use iBooks Author to create interactive books based on one of the library's special collections or exhibits.

- Have a program for teens and adults to learn how to create books using iBooks Author. Find a way to host and promote these books locally.

- Organize digital storytelling projects with the community using tools like iBooks Author for creating interactive books.

- Offer workshops for people who want to self-publish an app or interactive book. Begin with the easiest tools.

- Bring in experts to conduct workshops on how to create book apps.

- The library itself (or a consortium of libraries) could become a publisher of local digital content using iBooks Author to create interactive books.

- Work with faculty to develop interactive book apps for their courses and make these available in the library's digital repository.

- Host programs on writing fiction and nonfiction via interactive books and apps.

- Create local history apps that contain video interviews, maps, and photos—everything about the history of the local community.

Building Collections and Doing Reference

- Offer a collection of interactive book apps on iPads for loaning either inside the library or as take-home devices.

- Collect and categorize the best reference apps and put them on the iPads used by reference librarians. Use these reference apps to answer questions.

- Load reference book apps onto iPads and wander the building doing roving reference.

- Purchase print books that can be used with specific apps (virtual reality books), and make the iPad, the app, and the book available together.

- Work with other libraries to develop best practices for how libraries can deal with interactive book apps.

- Provide tablet stations where people can use tablets preloaded with excellent apps in different topic areas.

- Create iPad stations for children where they can try out interactive story apps. They can sit and read, have the app read to them, or have a parent or friend read to them.

- Advocate for better purchasing conditions for libraries. Advocate for better loaning contracts from publishers.

- Offer relevant apps on iPads in your "maker space"—apps that help with 3D printing and design.

- Embedded librarians could collect apps relevant to the communities they serve and store them on their own iPads for use when they are with their communities.

Reviewing Mobile Apps

- Contribute app reviews to the professional literature.
- Review more interactive book apps; start a blog about them; put information in a "staff picks" section and other special displays.
- Feature app reviews in a weekly column for the institution's newsletter or other publications.
- Review apps in library-related blogs.
- Include apps in bibliographies along with other types of resources.
- Create demo videos about useful apps for your users.
- Create reading lists of books that are in the form of book apps.
- Offer a "reader's advisory" service using book apps.

Professional Development

- Use apps to create your own resume, blog, or other website and to network with your colleagues via LinkedIn and at conferences and events.
- Use apps to manage your personal and professional social media accounts.
- Use apps for job searching and networking.
- Use apps for collecting and displaying information about events and conferences you are organizing.

How to Keep Up

If you feel like you're suffering from "app overload," you're not alone. The number of apps in Apple's and other app stores is increasing every day.[3] How do you keep up with finding out about the best apps in your area?

The iTunes App Store

One place that's worth checking on a regular schedule is Apple's App Store. Open iTunes on your Mac or Windows computer, or in the App Store on your iOS device to see what's new. Start by browsing in the "featured" category of best new apps. This is usually dominated by games, but also includes apps in other areas, such as reference or education. Look at any apps in your areas of interest, read the descriptions, look at the screen shots, and browse the reviews. Take the reviews with a grain of salt because anyone who purchases or downloads an app can review it, and many people dash off their thoughts without thinking or even using the app very much. It's more useful to search for reviews of the app from trusted sources and well-known websites, such as some of those mentioned in this chapter.

Apple features different collections of apps on a regular basis and sometimes those can be useful. Categories such as "grow your career" or "healthy living" might contain quality apps of interest. Look for a link called "app collections" to see a wide variety of specific collections of apps, put together by Apple, such as "start your business," "painting & drawing," or "apps for the great outdoors."

Next, tap on the "categories" list and choose from categories such as "books," "business," "education," "medical," "productivity," "reference," and more. Within each of those categories are similar subcategories as you find on the top level of the store—best new apps, essentials, and various featured collections and specific apps.

Also worth checking is the "top charts" section for the top paid and free apps in general and for each specific category. The "near me" button in the iOS version of the App Store shows you apps that are popular to your geographic location. This is a good way to discover apps about your local area, such as public transportation apps for your city.

If you are browsing the App Store on your iPhone, you'll see only iPhone apps, not iPad-only apps. For those, browse on your iPad or in iTunes on your computer. Remember that when you search in the app store on your iPad it defaults to iPad only, so if you're searching for an app that doesn't have an iPad version, you'll need to switch to the iPhone tab.

One more tip: if you know of an app that you particularly like, try tapping on the developer's name to see other apps made by them.

Specialized App Review Sites

One of my favorite app review sites is AppAdvice: http://appadvice.com. Particularly useful are their App Guides and App Lists. App Lists are specific collections of apps, such as Best iPad Apps for Artists or iPad Apps for Writers. App Guides are even more detailed collections, such as Spelling Study Aid Apps, Best GPS Activity Loggers, Best Apps for Learning Guitar, or Ocean Tide Apps. Within each specific list, the apps are grouped into three sections: Essential Apps, Notable Apps, and Decent Apps, with descriptions saying why they were chosen for each category.

Some app review sites are more specific, targeting a particular discipline. One such site is Medical App Journal: http://medicalappjournal.com/. Their slogan is "peer review for medical apps." They feature reviews by medical professionals, with links to their profiles on LinkedIn.[4] They display the top 200 apps in the Medical category of the iTunes store, and the titles in bold are the ones that have met their criteria, with links to reviews. Following specific sites like this one in areas of your interests is a good way to keep up.

App Reviews in Journals and Magazines That You Already Read

Whatever journals you currently read are likely reviewing apps in addition to books and other information sources. These are good ways to find out about new apps and also are a good place to consider submitting reviews of your own.

Google Alerts for App Reviews

You can also set up Google Alerts[5] for app reviews on specific topics you're interested in. Search for a topic like "iPad apps for architects" and have the results sent to you by e-mail or RSS feed once a day, once a week, or "as it happens."

Librarians as App Reviewers

I'd like to encourage more librarians to review apps. See the section in this book, Reviewing Apps: A Checklist, for tips and ideas on how to review apps.

Books

Brisbin, Shelly. *iOS Access for All: Your Comprehensive Guide to Accessibility for iPad, iPhone, and iPod Touch*. Shelly Brisbin, 2014.[6]

This book is a comprehensive look at the accessibility features of iOS devices. It's available in EPUB format, optimized for Apple's iBooks reader and tagged to provide maximum accessibility for screen readers. It includes detailed descriptions of how to use all the built-in accessibility features, how they work in Apple's apps, and a chapter on the best third-party apps that are accessible.

Carlson, Jeff. *The iPad Air and iPad Mini Pocket Guide*. San Francisco: Peachpit Press, 2014.[7]

Good book for beginners, for an overview of the basic functions of your iPad. The author has written many helpful technology books over the years.

Chen, Brian X. *Always On: How the iPhone Unlocked the Anything-Anytime-Anywhere Future—and Locked Us In.* New York: Da Capo Press, 2012.[8]

> Chen discusses both the positive and negative effects of being "always on" with our mobile devices. Recommended.

Harvell, Ben. *iConnected: Use AirPlay, iCloud, Apps, and More to Bring Your Apple Devices Together.* Indianapolis: Wiley, 2013.[9]

> Useful instructions for using your devices together, such as displaying your iPhone on an HDTV and effectively using iCloud for synchronization.

Hennig, Nicole, and Pam Nicholas. *Best Apps for Academics: A Guide to the Best Apps for Education and Research.* 2014. http://bestappsforacademics.com/.

> A guide to the best apps for students and professors in the categories of productivity; reading and annotating; research and reference; taking notes, writing, and studying; collaboration and sharing; presenting, lecturing, and publishing; discipline-specific examples and guides; and further resources.

Hennig, Nicole. *Selecting and Evaluating the Best Mobile Apps for Library Services.* Library Technology Reports, American Library Association, 2014 (forthcoming).

> Discusses mobile app technologies, natural user interfaces, accessibility, guidelines for evaluating and reviewing mobile apps, and ideas for integrating them into library services.

Kelly, Brett. *Evernote Essentials: The Definitive Guide for New Evernote Users,* 4th ed. Fullerton, CA: Brett Kelly Media, 2014.[10]

> Learn the best practices for using Evernote in useful and creative ways. Tips for beginners and for power users.

Kissell, Joe. *Take Control of Working with Your iPad,* 2nd ed. Ithaca, NY: TidBITS, 2011.[11]

> Focused on using the iPad for work. Covers creation of documents, spreadsheets, and presentations; and how to transfer files between devices, manage your calendars, take notes effectively, and print from your iPad. See also: "Take Control Live: Working with Your iPad"—video presentations by Joe Kissell (available for purchase)[12] with a document containing notes for each video. Includes apps for notes, documents, sharing, and useful power tips.

Lankes, R. David. *Expect More: Demanding Better Libraries for Today's Complex World.* [S.l.]: R. David Lankes, 2012.[13]

This excellent book is written for library users and stakeholders to get them thinking about the potential of libraries. Use with your communities to encourage discussions about how libraries are more than storehouses of books. This book is also available for free on the web: https://medium.com/p/c9efcfa6bd24.

Leibowitz, David Scott. *Mobile Digital Art: Using the iPad and iPhone as Creative Tools.* New York: Focal Press, 2013.[14]

An inspiring look at 70 different artists who use the iPhone or iPad to create digital art. Includes step-by-step instructions on how the works were created, with full-color illustrations. It includes painters, photographers, and artists who create collages, photomontage, abstract, and conceptual art.

Levin, Michal. *Designing Multi-device Experiences: An Ecosystem Approach to Creating User Experiences Across Devices.* Sebastopol, CA: O'Reilly, 2014.[15]

In our multi-device world, people often switch between smartphones, tablets, computers, wearables, and televisions to accomplish a task. This book combines theory and practice, offering many real-world examples in a highly readable way. These principles can be applied to designing better experiences for library users.

Marcolina, Dan. *iPhone Obsessed: Photo Editing Experiments with Apps.* Berkeley, CA: Peachpit Press, 2011.[16]

Excellent and fun book about using your iPhone to capture and edit images. Shows artwork and discusses apps used to create each piece.

Miller, Rebecca K., Heather Moorefield-Lang, and Carolyn Meier. *Rethinking Reference and Instruction with Tablets*, eEditions eBook. Chicago: ALA Editions, 2013.[17]

Firsthand accounts of library projects using tablets for reference and instruction.

Miller, Rebecca K., Heather Moorefield-Lang, and Carolyn Meier. *Tablet Computers in the Academic Library*, eEditions eBook. Chicago,: ALA Editions, 2014.[18]

Case studies and best practices for using tablets in the academic library and classroom.

Nichols, Joel A. *iPads in the Library: Using Tablet Technology to Enhance Programs for All Ages*. Santa Barbara, CA: Libraries Unlimited, 2013.[19]

> Specific programs and projects for use with iPads or other tablets. Includes projects for children, teens, and adults. Each project lists the apps needed, planning notes, and detailed instructions for the activity.

Pogue, David. *iPhone: The Missing Manual*, 7th ed. Sebastopol, CA: O'Reilly, 2013.[20]

> An easy reference for those new to the iPhone. Full of practical tips. Look for possible newer editions that match your iPhone at the time you read this.

Smith, Kei. *Digital Outcasts: Moving Technology Forward without Leaving People Behind*. Waltham, MA: Morgan Kaufmann, 2013.[21]

> A digital outcast is a term for those who are left behind the innovation curve of new technology for multiple reasons. This is an excellent book for gaining a nuanced approach to how we define and view people with "disabilities," and makes the point that we are all disabled (or will be) in one way or another at different points in our lives. It includes a detailed overview of how people with disabilities use technology, and it shows how creating accessible interfaces benefits everyone.

Sparks, David. *iPad at Work*. Hoboken, NJ : Wiley, 2011.[22]

> Excellent recommendations, tutorials, workflows, and advice about using your iPad for work.

Walsh, Andrew. *Using Mobile Technology to Deliver Library Services: A Handbook*. Lanham, MD: Scarecrow Press, 2012.[23]

> Examples and case studies of using mobile technology in academic libraries.

Blogs and Websites

The following apps, blogs, and websites are a good way to keep up with new apps of quality.

Androidapps Review. http://www.androidappsreview.com/.

> Full reviews of Android apps in categories such as Books, Business, Education, Medical, Music, News, and more.

Android Tapp. http://www.androidtapp.com/.

Reviews of Android apps in categories such as Finance, Health and Fitness, Multimedia, Music, News and Weather, Photography, Reference, Travel, and more.

AppAdvice. http://appadvice.com/.

Contains iPhone/iPad news, reviews, lists and guides to the best apps by function, such as flight tracker, apps to replace your camera, personal databases, Google Docs managers, and more.

Appstart for iPhone. https://itunes.apple.com/us/app/appstart-for-iphone/id488613223?mt=8.

Free iPhone app for browsing "starter kits," apps for getting started in each category.

Apptography. http://appotography.com/.

The world of photography apps is huge. Since photography can be used in so many ways as part of an academic's life, this is a good blog to follow for keeping up with the best photography apps. Covers iPhone, iPad, Mac, camera add-ons, and more.

Beautiful Pixels. https://beautifulpixels.com/.

If you care about excellent user interface design, this is the blog to follow. They select and review apps with outstanding design features. Covers apps for iPhone, iPad, Mac, Android, web, and more.

Macrumors Buyer's Guide. http://buyersguide.macrumors.com/.

If you are wondering when is the best time to buy or upgrade your iOS devices, visit this buyer's guide. For each device (iPhone, iPad, iPad mini, iPod Touch, iPod Shuffle, iPod Nano, iPod Classic), you can find out when it was last updated, so you can avoid buying a new device right before a new version. For each device they recommend: "buy now, product just updated," "neutral—mid-product cycle," or "don't buy—updates soon." They also provide details such as photos of the device, last release date, number of days since update, and links to rumors sites about upcoming releases.

Macworld App Guide. http://www.macworld.com/category/ios-apps/.

Reliable site containing app reviews for iOS devices.

Touch Press Blog. http://www.touchpress.com/blog/.

Publisher of beautiful interactive book apps for iPad, such as *The Elements, Beethoven's 9th Symphony,* and *Leonardo da Vinci Anatomy.* Follow them to keep up with their new titles.

Articles

The following articles are recommended for learning more about the topics in this book and may also be useful when you need to make a case for the importance of putting resources into learning more about mobile technologies.

1. Success Stories of Mobile Apps for Education

Barseghian, Tina. "How Can We Maximize the Potential of Learning Apps?" Mind/Shift - KQED. http://blogs.kqed.org/mindshift/2014/01/how-can-we-maximize-the-potential-of-learning-apps/ (accessed July 5, 2014).

This blog post is an excerpt from the book *The App Generation: How Today's Youth Navigate Identity, Intimacy, and Imagination in a Digital World,* by Howard Gardner and Katie Davis. Discusses the potential for each person to be a creator of knowledge and to make use of multiple forms of intelligence.

Carey, Jennifer. "iPad Summit Keynote Day 2: Ruben Puentedura." Indiana Jen blog. http://indianajen.com/2013/11/15/ipad-summit-keynote-day-2-ruben-puentedura/ (accessed July 5, 2014).

A summary by Carey of a presentation by Ruben Puentedura at the iPad Summit. Discusses why the iPad is special and useful for education—ubiquity, intimacy, embeddedness, curiosity amplifier, participatory culture, and more.

Cheng, Jacqui. "I Was an iPad Skeptic." Ars Technica. http://arstechnica.com/gadgets/2013/04/i-was-an-ipad-skeptic/ (accessed July 5, 2014).

Thoughts on the role of tablets in our lives and how they are different and better than first expected.

Dunn, Jeff. "Why Mobile Learning Is Inevitable." Edudemic. http://www.edudemic.com/why-mobile-learning-is-inevitable/ (accessed July 5, 2014).

Summary of a presentation called "Mobile Is Eating the World," by Benedict Evans (slides included), with many useful statistics that show why the future is mobile.

Kamenetz, Anya. "Three Student Successes with iPads." Digital/Edu Blog by the Hechinger Report. http://digital.hechingerreport.org/content/three-student-successes-with-ipads_973/ (accessed July 5, 2014).

Summaries of student successes, including second graders as tech experts, a shy student participating, and a disruptive student learning from screencasting his math-problem-solving ability.

Penny, Laurie. "Internet Detox Promotes the Myth of Web Toxicity." *Guardian*. http://www.theguardian.com/commentisfree/2013/may/06/the-myth-of-web-toxicity (accessed July 5, 2014).

The digital and physical worlds overlap and it's time to abandon the idea that technology can "corrupt your soul."

Popper, Ben. "Is Technology Scrambling My Baby's Brain?" The Verge. http://www.theverge.com/2013/9/3/4660216/is-technology-scrambling-my-babys-brain (accessed July 5, 2014).

A balanced approach to parenting of young children—focusing on the difference between passive and active consumption and reducing worry about new technologies.

Wainwright, Ashley. "8 Studies Show iPads in the Classroom Improve Education." SecurEdge Blog. http://www.securedgenetworks.com/secure-edge-networks-blog/bid/86775/8-Studies-Show-iPads-in-the-Classroom-Improve-Education (accessed July 5, 2014).

Summaries of and links to eight different studies on topics such as improved literacy rates, higher test scores, enhanced learning experiences, and better math skills.

2. Statistics on Mobile Use

Clark, Wilma, and RosemaryLuckin. "What the Research Says: iPads in the Classroom." London Knowledge Lab. http://digitalteachingand learning.files.wordpress.com/2013/03/ipads-in-the-classroom-report-lkl.pdf (accessed July 5, 2014).

Useful research report from the UK, with implications for decision makers and different user groups.

Columbus, Louis. "IDC: 87% of Connected Devices Sales by 2017 Will Be Tablets and Smartphones." *Forbes*. http://www.forbes.com/sites/louis columbus/2013/09/12/idc-87-of-connected-devices-by-2017-will-be -tablets-and-smartphones/ (accessed July 5, 2014).

Summary of statistics from IDC, including that tablets will outsell desktop and laptop PCs later in 2014.

May, Kevin. "Mobile Web Accounts for Just a Fifth of Time Spent on Devices, Apps Reign Supreme." TNooz.

http://www.tnooz.com/article/mobile-web-accounts-for-just-a-fifth-of -time-spent-on-devices-apps-reign-supreme/ (accessed July 5, 2014).

Useful summary of ComScore statistics, focusing on how users tend to stick with the app instead of the web version of popular sites, like Facebook.

"NMC Horizon Report: 2014 Higher Education Edition." NMC (New Media Consortium) and EDUCAUSE. http://www.nmc.org/publications/ 2014-horizon report-higher-ed (accessed July 5, 2014).

This useful in-depth report comes out every year. In the 2014 edition, read about "The Shift from Students as Consumers to Students as Creators," "The Growing Ubiquity of Social Media," and more. The 2013 report included information on the rise of tablet computing (also available on their website).

"Pew: More Americans Using Smartphones for Internet." Digital Book World. http://www.digitalbookworld.com/2013/pew-more-americans -using-smartphones-for-internet/ (accessed July 5, 2014).

Summary of Pew statistics, including that the proportion of U.S. adults who use smartphones to access the Internet has doubled since 2009 to 63 percent.

Purcell, Kristen, Alan Heaps, and Linda Friedrich. "How Teachers Are Using Technology at Home and in Their Classrooms." Pew Research Internet Project. http://www.pewinternet.org/2013/02/28/how-teachers -are-using-technology-at-home-and-in-their-classrooms/ (accessed July 5, 2014).

This report includes information about the use of mobile devices in the classroom, such as that 73 percent of teachers surveyed said that they or their students use mobile phones in the classroom to complete assignments. Discusses benefits and challenges of these technologies.

Radwanick, Sarah. "ComScore Introduces Mobile Metrix 2.0, Revealing That Social Media Brands Experience Heavy Engagement on Smartphones." http://www.comscore.com/Insights/Press_Releases/2012/5/Introducing _Mobile_Metrix_2_Insight_into_Mobile_Behavior (accessed July 5, 2014).

> A report with many statistics about mobile use, including that approximately 82 percent of time spent with mobile media happens via apps.

"Report: Teens and Technology 2013." Youth and Media. http:// youthandmedia.org/report-teens-and-tech/ (accessed July 5, 2014).

> Summary of latest findings from Pew Research, including that 78 percent of teens now have a cellphone and 47 percent of them own smartphones.

"Zero to Eight: Children's Media Use in America 2013." Common Sense Media. http://www.commonsensemedia.org/research/zero-to-eight -childrens-media-use-in-america-2013 (accessed July 5, 2014).

> Based on surveys of parents of children ages 0–8 in the United States, this study shows how children's behavior has changed on the topics of books and reading, music, and the use of smartphones and tablets.

3. The Digital Divide

Bridle, James. "E-readers: The Best Way to Get the World's Children Reading." *Guardian*. http://www.theguardian.com/technology/2013/sep/ 08/ebooks-ereaders-worldreader-kade-ghana (accessed July 5, 2014).

> Discusses Worldreader.org, a nonprofit that distributes e-readers (with teacher training) to schools in Africa and Europe. They found that it was cheaper and more effective to supply e-readers than print books.

Davidson, Christina. "Open for Whom? Designing for Inclusion, Navigating the Digital Divide." HASTAC: Humanities, Arts, Science, and Technology Alliance and Collaboratory. http://www.hastac.org/blogs/ tinadavidson/2013/08/01/chapter-six-open-whom-designing-inclusion -navigating-digital-divide (accessed July 5, 2014).

> A discussion of a graduate-level class that explored what we mean by "the digital divide." Not only is it a by-product of old inequalities, but new inequalities are appearing. In spite of that, digital technology has its own enabling role to play and sometimes allows people to leapfrog over social inequalities.

Pratt Dawsey, Chastity. "More Schools Giving Kids iPads to Make the Most of Apps." *Detroit Free Press*. http://www.freep.com/article/20130812/NEWS06/308120023/ipad-schools-technology-learning (accessed July 5, 2014).

Stories of iPad use in Michigan schools and how teachers are using apps to enable creativity and participation in the "flipped classroom." Mentions funding from grants, bond funds, and budgets previously devoted to textbooks.

Schwartz, Katrina. "Internet Access for All: A New Program Targets Low-Income Students." Mind/Shift - KQED. http://blogs.kqed.org/mindshift/2013/03/internet-access-for-everyone-a-new-program-targets-low-income-students/ (accessed July 5, 2014).

Discusses the EveryoneOn program, which offers low-cost devices, Internet services, and digital literacy training to programs that serve low-income people around the United States.

Shumski, Daniel. "5 Programs Putting iPads in Students' Hands This Fall." Education Dive. http://www.educationdive.com/news/5-programs-putting-ipads-in-students-hands-this-fall/166937/ (accessed July 5, 2014).

A brief look at five programs in public schools around the United States along with where the funding came from.

4. Special Needs and Assistive Technologies

"Apps for the Deaf and Hearing Impaired." AppAdvice. http://appadvice.com/applists/show/apps-for-the-deaf (accessed July 5, 2014).

Annotated list of several useful apps for the hearing impaired and how they work.

Aquino, Steven. "Re-enabled: iOS's Impact on Those with Impairments Isn't Just a Marketing Slide; It's Profound." The Magazine. http://the-magazine.org/9/re-enabled (accessed July 5, 2014).

The author, who is legally blind, works with preschool children with special needs. He discusses how and why iPad is extremely empowering for students and staff, and how it keeps the kids engaged far more effectively than conventional tools.

Cameron, Jenna. "Winnipeg Student Uses iPad to Speak First Words." CBC News. http://www.cbc.ca/m/touch/canada/manitoba/story/1.1864750 (accessed July 5, 2014).

Story of a seven-year-old girl with a congenital disorder that prevents speaking and how she's communicating with her iPad, with apps such as Touchchat.

Dunn, Jeff. "New Film by Apple Showcases the 4 Most Powerful Apps." Edudemic.

http://www.edudemic.com/new-apple-video-shows-the-power-of-apps-in -developing-countries/ (accessed July 5, 2014).

Story of an app that controls prosthetic legs and feet, along with stories of a few other apps and how they are helping people in developing countries.

Hendren, Sara. "All Technology Is Assistive Technology: Six Dispositions for Designers on Disability." Medium. https://medium.com/thoughtful -design/a8b9a581eb62 (accessed July 5, 2014).

Makes the case that it's wrong to divide the world into disabled or not disabled and that we are all disabled in different ways and at different times in our lives. Encourages designers and everyone to pay more attention to disability matters, with six principles for designers.

"iOS. A Wide Range of Features for a Wide Range of Needs." Apple. http://www.apple.com/accessibility/ios/ (accessed July 5, 2014).

Apple's pages explaining accessibility features—a helpful, illustrated guide.

Kornowski, Liat. "How the Blind Are Reinventing the iPhone." *Atlantic*. http://www.theatlantic.com/technology/archive/2012/05/how-the-blind -are-reinventing-the-iphone/256589/ (accessed July 5, 2014).

Inspiring article about how the iPhone has turned out to be as revolutionary as braille for blind users. Specific stories with details of how and why the iPhone works so well.

5. The Future of User Interfaces—Mobile and Beyond

Anderson, Chris, and Michael Wolff. "The Web Is Dead: Long Live the Internet." *Wired*. http://www.wired.com/magazine/2010/08/ff_webrip/all/ (accessed July 5, 2014).

Interesting discussion of the move from the web to apps.

Brownlee, John. "How Flat Design Is Preparing iOS for the Gadgets of Tomorrow." http://www.fastcodesign.com/3020586/how-flat-design-is -preparing-ios-for-the-gadgets-of-tomorrow (accessed July 5, 2014).

A look at how Apple's flat design of iOS 7 is going to work well with the design of car systems (with large buttons) and watches, since with flat design icons can be resized by just expanding the colors at their edges and filling the remaining space. This will work well on curved displays, such as watches that wrap around your wrist. Flat design will also make it easier to move to 3D displays.

Colliander, James, Ian Fordham, and Aron Solomon. "Ten Themes That Will Define the Next Decade of EdTech." Betakit. http://www.betakit.com/ten -themes-that-will-define-the-next-decade-of-edtech/ (accessed July 5, 2014).

A prediction of themes defining the next decade in educational technology, including collaboration, mobile, open data, and more.

della Cava, Marco. "Beyond a Gadget: Google Glass Is a Boon to the Disabled." *USA Today.* http://www.usatoday.com/story/tech/2013/10/22/ google-glass-aids-disabled/3006827/ (accessed July 5, 2014).

Interesting story of how Google Glass is used by people with various disabilities, and how it reduces the time between intention and action, something useful to all users. Being hands-free and voice-activated, it's a very helpful device for many situations.

Holland, Beth. "5 Myths about Writing with Mobile Devices." Edudemic. http://www.edudemic.com/5-myths-about-writing-with-mobile-devices/ (accessed July 5, 2014).

Excellent article about how writing is not just keyboarding and word processing, but is much more, including the process of creating blogs, eBooks, and curated digital magazines, all of which are done easily with apps and mobile devices.

Lenaerts, Sven. "The Future of User Interfaces." Tuts+. http://webdesign .tutsplus.com/articles/the-future-of-user-interfaces—webdesign-13246 (accessed July 5, 2014).

An article for web designers (and interesting for all) about the move away from graphical user interfaces, toward natural user interfaces, and away from metaphors, like desktops, toward direct manipulation.

Louis, Tristan. "Your Body Is the Computer." *Forbes.* http://www.forbes .com/sites/tristanlouis/2013/07/27/after-mobile-your-body-is-the-computer/ (accessed July 5, 2014).

Looks at the trend toward glasses and watches as technology devices, and how we're moving away from PCs toward smartphones, and then toward other smart devices, more integrated with our bodies.

Mims, Christopher. "Why Every Gadget You Own Could Soon Take Voice Commands, Just Like Siri." Quartz.

http://qz.com/165767/nuance-every-gadget-you-own-could-soon-take-voice-commands-just-like-siri/ (accessed July 5, 2014).

The story of how Nuance (the company that currently powers Apple's Siri) is offering licensing to its voice-control system to consumer electronics manufacturers, which could affect everything from smart thermostats to cars.

Quintal, Ryan. "The End of Keyboards: A Question of 'When?' " Design Shack. http://designshack.net/articles/business-articles/the-end-of-keyboards-a-question-of-when (accessed July 5, 2014).

The keyboard era is coming to an end with the prevalence of pen inputs, touch screens, voice commands, and more.

Sawers, Paul. "The Future of Handwriting." The Next Web. http://thenextweb.com/insider/2013/08/30/the-future-of-handwriting/ (accessed July 5, 2014).

Is handwriting going away in favor of keyboarding? Yes and no, according to this article, which discusses several interesting apps that use handwriting.

Vanhemert, Kyle. "Why *Her* Will Dominate UI Design Even More than *Minority Report*." *Wired*. http://www.wired.com/design/2014/01/will-influential-ui-design-minority-report (accessed July 5, 2014).

Makes the case that the way technology is portrayed in the movie *Her*— discreet, subtle, and human centered—is where technology is headed, and that this is a new era of personalized, intelligent apps.

6. New Roles for Libraries—Libraries as More than Collections of Books

Batykefer, Erinn, Laura Damon-Moore, and Christina Jones. "Library as Incubator Project." http://www.libraryasincubatorproject.org/ (accessed July 5, 2014).

A site that advocates for libraries as incubators of the arts.

Chant, Ian. "Opening Up: Next Steps for MOOCs and Libraries." *Library Journal*. http://lj.libraryjournal.com/2013/12/digital-content/opening-up (accessed July 5, 2014).

Discusses an academic library offering its own MOOCs and a public library using a MOOC as the foundation of a summer reading program. Makes the case that libraries are well placed to be part of experiments with MOOCs.

Farkas, Meredith. "Libraries as Publishers: Our Push to Change the Publishing Landscape." American Libraries. http://www.american librariesmagazine.org/article/libraries-publishers (accessed July 5, 2014).

Exploring the role of libraries in enabling publishing, through publishing the work of the library's constituencies (public libraries) and through publishing open-access work (academic libraries). First of a series.

"Four Local Libraries Honored for Offering Cutting-Edge Services." Digital Book World. http://www.digitalbookworld.com/2014/four -libraries-offering-cutting-edge-digital-services/ (accessed July 5, 2014).

ALA honored four libraries offering cutting-edge technology services, including services for easy video creation by faculty and students, and using Instagram's API to capture photos tagged with the library's hashtag and display them online and in the library.

Godin, Seth. "The Future of the Library." Seth Godin's blog. http://sethgodin.typepad.com/seths_blog/2011/05/the-future-of-the -library.html (accessed July 5, 2014).

Describes librarians as people who can bring domain knowledge and access to information, helping users create and invent.

Morozov, Evgeny. "Making It: Pick Up a Spot Welder and Join the Revolution." *New Yorker*.

http://www.newyorker.com/arts/critics/atlarge/2014/01/13/140113crat _atlarge_morozov (accessed July 5, 2014).

Essay about the "maker movement," its history, and where it could go.

Nawotka, Edward. "A Visit to BibiloTech: The 21st Century All-Digital Library." Publishing Perspectives.

http://publishingperspectives.com/2014/01/a-visit-to-bibliotech-the-21st
-century-all-digital-library (accessed July 5, 2014).

> The story of an all-digital public library in San Antonio, Texas. They loan
> out e-readers for home use. Discusses how economical it was to build,
> compared to other public libraries with print collections.

> Peterson, Andrea. "Need to Use a 3-D Printer? Try Your Local Library."
> *Washington Post.*

http://www.washingtonpost.com/blogs/the-switch/wp/2013/08/01/need-
to-use-a-3-d-printer-try-your-local-library/ (accessed July 5, 2014).

> A story on library 3D printing services, focusing on the Martin Luther
> King Jr. Memorial Library in Washington, DC.

Peterson, Andrea. "Digital Age Is Forcing Libraries to Change."
Washington Post. http://www.washingtonpost.com/blogs/the-switch/wp/
2013/08/07/the-digital-age-is-forcing-libraries-to-change-heres-what
-that-looks-like/ (accessed July 5, 2014).

> All about the "digital commons" at the Martin Luther King Jr. Memorial
> Library in Washington, DC. Try out eBook readers, use a 3D printer, use
> the Skype station, a coworking space, and more.

Rendon, Frankie. "The Changing Landscape for Libraries & Librarians in
the Digital Age." TeachThought. http://www.teachthought.com/literacy-2/
changing-landscape-libraries-librarians-digital-age/ (accessed July 5,
2014).

> Discusses why libraries are more relevant than ever, with librarians
> offering digital services, technology training, and serving as key part-
> ners in community relations.

Resnick, Brian. "The Library of the Future Is Here." Business Insider.
http://www.businessinsider.com/library-of-the-future-2014-1 (accessed
July 5, 2014).

> Describes libraries not as warehouses of books, but as services and tools
> for the commons.

Sipley, Gina. "Surprise! It's the Golden Age of Libraries." PolicyMic.
http://www.policymic.com/articles/67457/surprise-it-s-the-golden-age
-of-libraries (accessed July 5, 2014).

> On reimagining the library as digital space, with books no longer the focal
> point.

Stinson, Susan. "Writers in Residence at Forbes Library: Three Programs." Library as Incubator Project. http://www.libraryasincubator project.org/?p=12843 (accessed July 5, 2014).

Local writer describes her experience as writer-in-residence at Forbes Library in Northampton, Massachusetts.

"Symposium: Creative Making for Libraries & Museums." Dysart & Jones. http://www.creativemaking.org/ (accessed July 5, 2014).

A symposium held in July 2013 that focused on creative making in libraries and museums, with examples of makerspaces, fab labs, and more.

Tennant, Roy. "The Mission of Librarians Is to Empower." The Digital Shift. http://www.thedigitalshift.com/2014/01/roy-tennant-digital-libraries/ mission-librarians-empowerment (accessed July 5, 2014).

Discusses many of the ways we empower our users and communities—increasing knowledge, providing access to tools, and more.

Notes

1. The Book as iPad App, my online course: http://apps4librarians.com/ bookapps/.
2. For example, here's a presentation I created for librarians at the Harvard Graduate School of Design on apps for architecture and urban planning: http:// www.slideshare.net/nic221/apps-for-architecture-urban-planning.
3. More than 1 million apps were available in Apple's store as of fall 2013. See this site for a list showing how it has grown year by year: http://ipod.about.com/ od/iphonesoftwareterms/qt/apps-in-app-store.htm.
4. Information about reviewers on Medical App Journal: http://www.medical appjournal.com/inner.php?id=3.
5. Set up Google Alerts: http://www.google.com/alerts.
6. iOS Access for All: http://www.iosaccessbook.com/.
7. http://www.worldcat.org/oclc/859556364.
8. http://www.worldcat.org/oclc/827209745.
9. http://www.worldcat.org/oclc/820108777.
10. Evernote Essentials: http://www.amazon.com/Evernote-Essentials -Definitive-Guide-Users-ebook/dp/B00KE9ZBII/.
11. http://www.worldcat.org/oclc/741364948.
12. Take Control Live: Working with Your iPad (video presentations): http:// www.takecontrolbooks.com/tclive-working-ipad.
13. http://www.worldcat.org/oclc/797017489.
14. http://www.worldcat.org/oclc/826123121.
15. http://www.worldcat.org/oclc/852807810.
16. http://www.worldcat.org/oclc/682896805.
17. http://www.alastore.ala.org/detail.aspx?ID=10861.

18. http://www.alastore.ala.org/detail.aspx?ID=4025.
19. http://www.worldcat.org/oclc/816512996.
20. http://shop.oreilly.com/product/0636920029052.do.
21. http://www.worldcat.org/oclc/835600879.
22. http://www.worldcat.org/oclc/760015268.
23. http://www.worldcat.org/oclc/810119077.

Glossary

Accelerometer: An accelerometer is an electronic component that measures tilt and motion. A device with an accelerometer knows what angle it is being held at. It can also measure movements such as rotation, and motion gestures such as swinging, shaking, and flicking. One common use in smartphones is to detect whether the phone is upright or sideways, and to automatically rotate the graphics on the screen accordingly. Another common use is for controlling games and other applications (such as a music player) by moving or shaking the phone.

AirPlay: AirPlay (http://www.apple.com/airplay/) is Apple's technology for wirelessly streaming audio, video, or photos between devices. For example, an iPhone can stream audio from a number of different music or radio apps to an Apple TV on the same Wi-Fi network. Another use would be to play a video you just shot on your iPhone to the large-screen TV hooked up to Apple TV of a friend that you are visiting.

Bluetooth: Bluetooth is a short-range wireless technology used to pair gadgets that are near each other. For example, you can pair your mobile phone with a Bluetooth speaker to play music wirelessly. It's also used to pair your mobile device with a wireless keyboard, or to send photos or other files from one mobile device to another. Most laptops are also enabled with Bluetooth technology.

EPUB (and other eBook formats): EPUB is an open standard for eBooks. Files have the extension *.epub*. It's designed for creating reflowable and resizable text. It's supported by a wide variety of e-readers and e-reading apps (such as iBooks, Nook, or Kobo), with the exception of Amazon's Kindle, which uses the MOBI or AZW format. Other eBook formats to be aware of include: iBOOKS (the format used by Apple for multimedia eBooks created with iBooks Author) and PDF ("portable document format"—an electronic image of text and graphics designed to look the same as the printed page). File extensions for these formats are *.epub, .mobi, .azw, .ibooks, .pdf.*

In-app purchase: This refers to the ability to purchase additional features within either a paid or free app. For example, games often are set up so you can buy more levels within the game for extra money. Painting and drawing apps often allow the purchase of extra virtual pens and brushes this way.

In-app browser: Many apps have a web browser built into them, so that when you follow a link to a website, you don't need to leave the app and go to your mobile device's browser (such as Safari). News readers, such as Reeder or Feedly, often use in-app browsers so that you can read the full story from a news feed without leaving the app.

iOS: Apple's operating system that runs on iPhone, iPod Touch, iPad, and Apple TV.

Jailbreaking: Jailbreaking refers to modifying Apple's iOS in order to install apps other than the those that are approved by Apple in the iTunes store. It allows you to run unofficial code, such as themes, hacks, and apps that add functionality. Despite the name, it is legal to jailbreak your iPhone[1] (but not your iPad).[2] See the section in this book: Jailbreaking: What Librarians Should Know.

Location awareness: Location awareness is the ability to show information about the physical location of a device. The most familiar example is in mapping apps, like Google Maps, where you can tap an icon to see where you currently are on the map. It's also used in apps like Foursquare that allow you to "check in" to a restaurant, park, or store, in order to show your friends where you are and read and write reviews of local places. It has many other uses, such as geotagging your photos, making a map of your walk, bike ride, or hike, and tracking a lost mobile device or laptop.

Multi-touch: Multi-touch refers to the ability of a touch screen or trackpad to recognize the presence of multiple points of contact. It's used for technology such as "pinch to zoom" or two-finger scrolling to control your device.

Native app vs. web app: A native app is an app that has been designed to run on specific mobile devices and is purchased or downloaded from an app store. It can take advantage of all of the device's features (accelerometer, gestures, and so on), and it can be designed to work offline.

Mobile web apps are apps that run inside a mobile web browser. They are built with standards-based technologies such as HTML5 and CSS3. You can find them as you would find any website, and then "install" them on your home screen by saving a bookmark to the site.

Developers often prefer mobile web apps, since they need to be created only once, and then can run on all platforms with modern standards-based browsers. Users often prefer native apps, since they are easy to find (just search the app store), usually run faster, have been vetted to make sure they are free of security issues (in Apple's case), and provide the best user experience.[3]

Skeuomorphism: Skeuomorphism is a design practice that involves using ornamental elements of past iterations of an object, such as wood bookshelves in an e-reading app or calendars with faux-leather stitching in a calendar app. In the early days of mobile app design, this was used often, but it has now fallen out of favor. When a technology is new, skeuomorphism is used as a mental aid, to make new technology feel familiar by imitating physical objects.

Universal app: A universal app is designed so that you need to purchase it only once and it will be optimized to run on both the iPhone and iPad, in a way that suits the display size of each device.

Notes

1. http://www.engadget.com/2010/07/26/library-of-congress-adds-dmca-exception-for-jailbreaking-or-root/.
2. http://www.businessinsider.com/jailbreak-the-iphone-but-not-the-ipad-2012-10.

3. For more details, see "The Pros and Cons of Native Apps and Mobile Web Apps" at http://mobiledevices.about.com/od/additionalresources/qt/The-Pros-And-Cons-Of-Native-Apps-And-Mobile-Web-Apps.htm. Some predict that web apps will win in the end; see "Why Web Apps Will Crush Native Apps" at http://mashable.com/2012/09/12/web-vs-native-apps/. Others encourage a focus on native apps; see "Hybrid Apps vs. Native Apps: The Verdict Is In, Go Native and Give Users Something They Will Love" at http://tapsense.com/blog/2013/09/30/hybrid-apps-vs-native-app-the-verdict-is-in-go-native-and-give-your-users-something-theyll-love/.

Alphabetical List of Apps

The following is a list of all the apps mentioned in this book. Apps in bold are featured with full descriptions: others are mentioned in the "Other Apps Worth Trying" sections.

About the Author

NICOLE HENNIG is an independent user experience professional, helping librarians and educators effectively use mobile technologies. Her online courses, "Apps for Librarians and Educators" and "The Book as iPad App," have enabled librarians from all types of institutions to effectively implement mobile apps in their programs and services. She worked as webmaster and head of user experience for the MIT Libraries for 14 years. Her awards include the MIT Libraries Infinite Mile Award for Innovation and Creativity, the MIT Excellence Award for Innovative Solutions, and the ASIS&T Chapter Member of the Year. Visit her website at http://nicolehennig.com.

To stay current with mobile technologies, sign up for Nicole's newsletter, Mobile Apps News, at http://nicolehennig.com/mobile-apps-news/.

More by Nicole Hennig

Best Apps for Academics: A Guide to the Best Apps for Education and Research by Nicole Hennig and Pam Nicholas.
http://bestappsforacademics.com/

This book is for students and professors who would like to make best use of smartphones and tablets in their academic work. If you already use your preinstalled apps but haven't had time to explore many other apps, then this book is for you.

- We point you to the *best* apps so you won't have to wade through the millions of apps available in today's app stores (many of varying quality).

- We focus on apps for Apple's iOS and Google's Android platforms.

- We cover apps that could be used by academics in many different disciplines.

- The book includes specific examples of how academics are using these apps in their work.

Online Courses

Apps for Librarians and Educators
http://apps4librarians.com/

This course is available via Simmons Graduate School of Library and Information Science (GSLIS) continuing education for six-week sessions online or in a self-study version[1] that you can purchase anytime and complete at your own pace.

The course covers the best apps in several categories, such as reading, productivity, reference, and multimedia. Each week's lesson includes screencast demos of apps, provocative readings, discussion questions, and an optional live chat. You'll learn how to write app reviews and you'll share them with your colleagues in a private class blog.

Testimonials

"Before taking Apps4Librarians, I didn't realize there were so many apps that could be useful in educational settings. I look forward to sharing information about some of the apps I learned about in this course with my colleagues and possibly lead some workshops on specific apps."

—Ellen Lutz, Research Services Librarian in the Sciences, University of Texas at San Antonio

"Excellent course. This class exceeded my expectations. It provided a good mix of the practical and theoretical components of iOS and android applications. Nicole is enthusiastic, encouraging, engaging and very knowledgeable."

—Maryjane Canavan, Head of Library Systems, University of Massachusetts, Amherst

The Book as iPad App

http://apps4librarians.com/bookapps/

This course is available via the American Library Association for six-week sessions online or in a self-study version[2] that you can purchase anytime and complete at your own pace. It's useful for anyone who cares about the future of the book and the blurring boundaries between book and app.

The course covers multimedia, multi-touch eBooks—the kind that are published as individual apps. We look at fiction, nonfiction, reference, children's books, and graphic novels. These book apps include many features that are useful for education, such as embedded videos, slide-shows, quizzes, and more.

Each week's lesson includes screencast demos of apps, provocative readings, discussion questions, and an optional live chat. You'll learn how to write app reviews and you'll participate in group brainstorming sessions about how these apps can be used in library programs and services. By the end, you'll be familiar with what makes the best interactive reading experience and you'll be inspired with ideas for library programs using these apps.

Testimonial

"This four-week course gets five stars not only for the information it contains, but also for the level of empowerment it provides. I signed up not knowing a thing about book apps, and in a month's time I am using them at work and collaborating with a library colleague to create a book app of our own for use in story times. The topic is timely, relevant and fun! I couldn't ask for more."

—Susan Hansen, Branch Manager, West Hartford Public Library, Hartford, CT

Notes

1. Self-study version of Apps for Librarians & Educators online course: https://www.udemy.com/apps4librarians/?couponCode=APPS4LIB-BOOK.
2. Self-study version of The Book as iPad App online course: https://www.udemy.com/bookapps/?couponCode=APPS4LIB-BOOK.